With or Without You?

Eleven units on Relationships for young people aged 14+

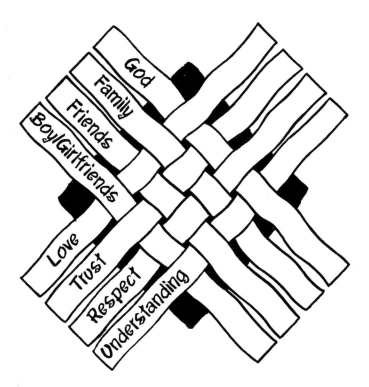

ACKNOWLEDGEMENTS

Material written and prepared by Liz West and Elaine Williams
after much discussion with David Fowler, Liz Potter and Sue Sinclair!

Typesetting, artwork and design by Matthew Slater

Special thanks are due to...
   ... Terry Dunnell, for his helpful comments and observations
   ... Tony Ralph and Keith Bernhardt, for proof-reading the final texts
   ... Keith Mitchell and the young people of Yatton Crusaders, for their help in trying out the material
   ... Anne Carlos at CITS, for providing the statistics, quotes and additional resources.

The structure of this course was inspired by Tom Marshall's book, 'Right Relationships' (Sovereign World, 1989).

Printed and bound in the United Kingdom by Stanley L Hunt (Printers) Ltd., Rushden, Northants.

Scriptures quoted from the New Century Version (Anglicised Edition)
Copyright © 1993 by Nelson Word Ltd, 9 Holdom Avenue, Bletchley, Milton Keynes, MK1 1QR, UK.

Crusaders, 2 Romeland Hill, St. Albans, AL3 4ET.

With or Without You?

Contents

Are you wondering what you have let yourself in for in choosing this course?

Your young people need to be able to talk about relationships in a Christian atmosphere - after all, they are being talked about everywhere else! They will already have formed opinions on many of the key issues, but still very much need opportunities to test what God has to say.

You are not expected to be an expert yourself, and you don't have to be personally successful in all the aspects covered by the course - none of us are!! You just need a desire to help your young people in this important area of their lives. We've learned so much as we have put this material together and hope that you also will deepen your understanding of relationships as you use it with your group. Things <u>are</u> very different now from when you were their age (if you are older than 25!), so don't assume anything as you go into this course - or be shocked by anything for that matter. The important thing is to be open and honest and not to dodge the issues as they come up.

So... we invite you to take your courage in both hands and plunge in, with the expectation that you **will** see growth and change in your group!

We are wanting your young people to build up a complete picture of relationships, beginning with how they see themselves and then reaching out to friends and family, the opposite sex, those in authority... and God Himself. As your young people focus on love, trust, honour, respect, and understanding - the key elements which build successsful relationships - they will be challenged to take what they learn and apply it to their own lives and situations.

We hope this will have an effect for a long time to come.

An overview

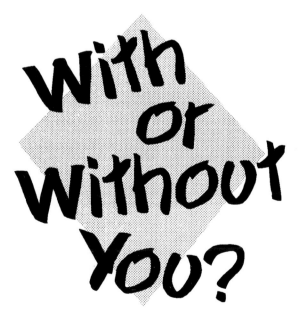

Four blocks.... We recommend that you take breaks through the course for a social gathering or activity - one after unit 3, one after unit 6 and one after unit 9.

....of eleven units The material in each unit is written as a sequence, with one activity following on from the next, but you may need several sessions to cover just one unit! Don't be tempted to cram the sessions full - your young people will gain most from being able to go into the different parts in depth.. and that takes time! You are in the best position to judge which aspects of the course are most relevant to your young people... and to know when to stop a session. You will want to keep things moving without rushing them, and yet be flexible enough to put your agenda aside if something important comes up.

When you do break a unit, perhaps start with your own 'icebreaker' the following week and then a summary of the previous session, which will lead you into picking up where you left off. This flexibility should enable your group to go at the right speed for its members and still ensure that the whole course is covered.

A Unit Explained

The aims for the unit

Summary of the unit, showing you 'routes' through the material, to help you plan.

Title

What you will need for this activity - underlined items need to be prepared in advance!

Shows how this activity fits into the overall picture. We use different kinds of activity (discussion, drama, role-play, creative Bible study....) to get the young people involved.

Continuation arrow - there may be more to the activity over the page!

Within the illustrated page:

BREAK THE ICE

OPINION-MAKERS
Part 1: What everybody else says...

Part 2: What I say...

Part 3: What the Bible says...

Level One   Level Two   Level Three

NEXT...

Option A   Option B

FOCUS AND ACT

We want our young people to...

- know that sex is part of God's creation, which He intended for our pleasure

- be absolutely clear about God's guidelines for sexual behaviour

- be aware that society, the media and some of their peers will be following a different pattern - and that there will be pressure to do the same!

5. A more Excellent Way

Break the ice

The idea is... to get the young people to begin to think about who influences their opinions about sex - and how.

YOU WILL NEED
To brief 4 or 5 young people
A cassette player

In advance, ask 4 or 5 young people to record onto tape a recent song which contains something about romantic or sexual love. Ask them also to write the lyrics out large on a piece of paper (and not to mention which song they have chosen to other group members before the session!)

1. EITHER Karaoke - have extroverts sing to the songs as they are played on the tape.

   OR Guess - have the young person who has chosen the song read out the lyrics, line by line - ask the rest of the group to try to identify the song, and play it (or part of it) once they have guessed correctly.

2. Display all the lyrics.

47

We've identified **three levels** of spiritual understanding, in the hope that your young people will be taken forward from wherever they are now.

Level One

is for those who may not be aware that they are spiritual beings at all - they will be encouraged to start thinking in this way as well as increasing their understanding of how relationships work.

Level Two

is for those who might have information about God but who you feel do not yet have a personal relationship with Him. They will find that applying the principles of the Bible's teaching makes sense - and that it works.

Level Three

is for those who know God as Father, Saviour and friend - they will be encouraged to apply Godly values to their lives from the Bible, with a degree of accountability in this.

If you feel your young people are all at different stages, then maybe you will need to discuss with them where they feel they are and have different small groups for each stage. It should be possible to use the material in this way, although feedback times after small group activities will need a bit of thinking through!

But first... Find out what's going on...

It's important that you, as leader, are aware of the influences on your young people from the culture that they live in. This is the time to brush up on the kind of music they listen to, what magazines they read and favourite TV programmes they watch. If you keep doing this through the course you will find plenty of examples of things that are relevant, especially in the 'soaps'. You will know that many of their opinions will be influenced by the world they live in and not by Biblical teaching. It would also be helpful for you to know something about the family background of your young people, so that you can treat issues sensitively. Some aspects of the course might bring things to the surface which will be painful, and you would do well to be prepared.

Setting the Scene

Each time the group meets your aim as a leader should be to encourage deeper relationships among the group members, enabling confidence to be built up and so facilitate learning and sharing and growth in the individuals. Seemingly unimportant things can influence this process - how you set up the room, for example, so that there can be eye contact in group discussions. Even the refreshments you provide and how you greet the young people will have an influence!

Confidentiality is vital. At the beginning of the course, emphasise that nothing should be shared with people who are not part of the group, and remind them of this as often as you feel is necessary. Some people ask their young people to sign an written agreement to add weight to this. It is also important that all group members will be able to contribute to group discussions without fear of ridicule. You may feel that you need to make this point at the beginning as well, on the basis that everyone's contribution is valid.

Leading a Discussion

People learn much more from discussing questions and arriving at their own conclusions than by being told all the answers. Questions that provoke discussion are those which do not have a 'yes' or 'no' answer - questions which start with 'what', 'who', 'when', 'how', for example. You must then be prepared for the silence to follow as people think out their contribution. After the first few replies you could respond with an "uh-huh" or "yes", showing that the answer is valid, but that you expect more responses form others. "What else?" might encourage others to add their bit, and then a final "Is there anything else?"

Other general questions can be useful, such as, "What other ways are there of thinking about this?", "What do you think this means?", "What other ideas do people have along this line?", or "How can you apply this to your life?". In this way you will encourage the whole group to participate. Let it be said though that there is a great art in working out good questions, and preparation will help, as will practice. It's also helpful to summarise the group's conclusions as the discussion proceeds.

You'll also need to know how to draw out individuals who are silent and how to deal with the ones who talk too much. As a general rule, do not pick on people who have not contributed to the discussion - they may well take longer to feel at ease with the group, so it's wise to give them some space. You could ask them afterwards how they felt the discussion had gone and encourage them to share what they had got out of it. The difficulty of the over-talkative and the silent are better dealt with outside the group, on a one-to-one basis. You are aiming at achieving a relaxed atmosphere where people can be increasingly open as trust builds. Humour, but not at other people's expense, is a very good tool to use in this process.

One idea that has worked to encourage everyone to participate is give out three matches to each member. The young people then forfeit one match each time they speak - this really does seem to encourage the quiet ones to contribute, whilst obviously limiting the contributions of the over-talkative.

If you find that you are doing all the talking, it may be a good idea to have some social activities to help the group be more open. You could also ask beforehand for one of the group to lead a section and make sure you do not chip in.

Giving a Short Talk

There may be times when the best way for you to put over some information is simply by giving a talk. In order for these to be effective, there are some simple guidelines to follow:

➤ Think out what you want to say beforehand, but do not read from your notes
➤ Make sure what you say is short and to the point - no waffling on!
➤ Use humour as much as possible
➤ Make sure the language you use is 'teenage-friendly'
➤ Make what you say relevant by using examples your young people can relate to
➤ Try to encourage group members to think about what you are saying in relation to their own opinions and situations.

Afterwards, it's a good idea to check with some members of the group that you've communicated what you had intended, and be humble enough to accept any negative comments and learn from them!

Discipline

As with any group situation, you may want to think through what expectations you have about behaviour in the group and think of a way of communicating these expectations at the beginning of the course. There's no reason why you, as leader, should not be able to firmly set boundaries of acceptable behaviour. Be firm, but also be aware of the reasons behind certain behaviour: someone who is hurting a lot may want to deflect attention from a difficult area, and you may anticipate some embarrassed giggling in units 5 and 6.

You will need great wisdom in knowing how to respond to things you consider to be unacceptable. Remember that you will be modelling many of the principles in this course as you relate to the group as a whole and as individuals!

Increased ownership of the group by the young people will often deal with discipline problems and is an important principle in any youth work. As you get to know the individuals better, be aware of where their gifts and strengths lie: it would be particularly good during this course if you were to commit yourself to finding ways of developing these gifts, even though this will sometimes mean taking risks. It will probably mean allowing for things not to run quite so smoothly as usual, and this needs to be acceptable to the group - better to have tried and mucked up than never to have had a go! It's important to be really positive and encouraging, without, of course, going overboard and being misleading!

We suggest that you look through the programme and mark the parts which your young people could take on. Although we are used to leading, more and more in education and at work, young people are being trained to do things for themselves. They will learn so much more effectively when they have had to take responsibility, and the whole group will benefit.

As you work through this material with your group, you will undoubtedly touch issues which are major problems in the lives of some of your young people. It's really important that individuals can talk things through on a one-to-one basis: you will want to provide an opportunity for this at the end of each session, either by making yourself available, or by asking another leader to take on this role.

Young People in Difficulty

There may also be times when a young person will want to talk at length outside of group time. Whilst this is an encouraging sign of trust, it's good to remind ourselves not to get into intimate situations with a young person of the opposite sex. Be warned, youth leaders have run into problems in this area! It's useful to be part of a mixed leadership team so that you can help each other out.

It's quite common for youth leaders to feel out of their depth in knowing how to help a young person - here are a few guidelines:

➤ Do not be simplistic, gloss over difficulties, or pretend that 'everything will be alright' - it will be more helpful to the young person that you listen and really try to understand, than that you offer 'quick fix' solutions.

➤ A young person may ask you 'not to tell anybody', but do not promise to keep a secret before you know what the young person is going to share with you - it may be a problem which you will need to pass on to a professional agency. Explain this to the young person. If you feel you do need to involve others, talk this over **with the young person** and try to reach agreement about the action you will take - if the young person has trusted you enough to confide in you, they are usually happy to trust you with the next step.

➤ If in doubt, get advice!!! We have found CARE to be very helpful (see the RESOURCES pages at the back for details.)

And Finally...

We would encourage you to find those who will pray for you and for your group at all times, but particularly as you work through this course on relationships. These are mightily important issues, but remember that it is God's job to care for your young people and you are simply co-operating with Him in allowing an opportunity for the Holy Spirit to work. There is a little verse at the end of **1 Thessalonians 1, chapter 5**, which says *"The one who calls you is faithful and He will do it"*: may you and your young people draw nearer to God and enjoy your time together as you work through this course.

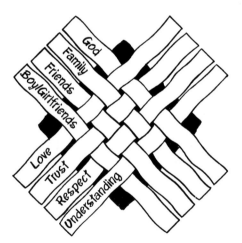

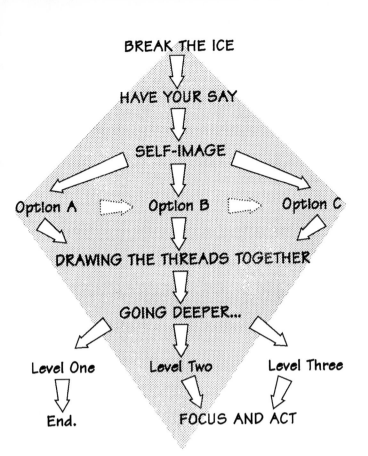

We want our young people to...

■ say what they would like to discuss and consider in this teaching series

■ be aware of their own self-image

■ understand that they are made up of body, mind, emotions *and* spirit *or* contrast this with facts about how God views them and act on the difference

1.Me

Break the ice

The idea is... that the young people will begin to think and talk about themselves in a light-hearted way.

YOU WILL NEED
A 3" X 5" card for
    each person
Pens

1. Give each person a card and a pen.

2. Ask everyone to imagine that they are going on a journey and then to write down (without letting others see):

   ➤ their chosen destination - anywhere in the world!
   ➤ who they would choose as a travelling companion (famous or not, dead or alive!)
   ➤ one cassette to listen to,
   ➤ three items they absolutely must have in their suitcase (not general eg clothes, but specific eg DM's),
   ➤ what or who they would miss most if they were away for any length of time.

   Make it clear from the outset that the rest of the group will hear what is being written down!

3. Ask everyone to sign their cards, and then collect them in.

4. Now read the cards out one by one and ask the group to guess who has written the card.

if **you would prefer a competitive team game...**
Ask the young people to make 2 teams and collect the cards in 2 separate piles. Taking a card from each pile in turn, read out a clue at a time and ask the opposite team to guess who has written the card. Award 5 points if they guess correctly after the first clue, 4 after the second and so on.

Have your say

The idea is... that the young people should have an opportunity to decide which issues will be dealt with in the following sessions.

YOU WILL NEED
Large sheets of paper
Thick, bold pens
Blu-tack

1. Point out that the emphasis in BREAK THE ICE was on ourselves, and that this will be the starting point for a series on RELATIONSHIPS...

2. Ask the young people to get into groups of 4, 5 or 6 and give each group a large piece of paper and a pen.

3. In these groups, ask them to note down any issues they would like to discuss under the title of relationships - give examples (how to get on with parents; sex; choosing **real** friends...) if necessary.

4. After 5 minutes, ask each group to tack its ideas sheet somewhere around the room.

5. Allow a few minutes for everyone to mill around and read all of the sheets.

6. Bringing the whole group back together again, make brief comments about which issues seemed important (and which may have been overlooked).

7. Keep the ideas sheets - make sure that you cover these questions and issues over this series and try to refer back to the sheets themselves from time to time!

Self-image

The idea is... that the young people begin to think about their self-image in more depth.

Choose the activity or activities which would work best with your group!

Option A: Hot seat

YOU WILL NEED
To make copies

In advance, photocopy pages 7 and 8, and cut along the dotted lines - you will need one whole set for every 4 to 6 young people you are expecting to come to the session.

1. Ask the young people to get into groups of 4, 5 or 6 - perhaps use the same groups as in HAVE YOUR SAY...

$\Rightarrow$

2. Give each group a set of cards and ask each group to establish one chair as a 'hot seat'.

3. Each person then takes it in turn on the 'hot seat' - the others in the group pick up 3 cards and read them out for the 'hot seater' to respond to (NB he/she may 'pass' on a question!)

4. Ask for quick feedback:

   ~ *Did you find it easy or difficult to talk about yourself like this?*
   ~ *Which questions were particularly difficult to answer?*
   ~ *Why do you think that this is so?* (Be prepared to say how you would feel on the 'hot seat'!)

   Briefly sum up what the young people have said.

Option B: Lonely hearts

YOU WILL NEED
Paper
Pens

1. Give each young person a pen and a piece of paper.

2. Ask everyone to write a 'lonely hearts' advert., concentrating on what they might say about themselves rather than about the person they might like to meet!

3. With a partner or in a threesome, allow some time for the young people to talk together about what has been written:

   ~ *How accurate is it?*
   ~ *What kind of things wouldn't you tell someone about yourself?*

Option C: What am I really like?

YOU WILL NEED
To make copies
Pens

In advance, make photocopies of page 9, enough for one per person.

1. Give each young person a copy of the sheet and a pen.

2. Ask everyone to:

   ➤ circle all the words which they think apply to them, adding words like 'sometimes' and 'very' as appropriate,
   ➤ look again at the circled words and put a line through those which they wish didn't apply to them and a star by those they are pleased about,
   ➤ underline the words which describe what they would like to be, but aren't.

3. You may like to allow some time for discussion in pairs or threes, focusing particularly on any differences between how individuals view themselves and how others see them.

Drawing the threads together

Sum up by commenting that:

➤ there are some things about ourselves which we like... some we don't
➤ there are some things about ourselves which we can change (eg hair colour, bad habits!)... others we can't (eg height, eye colour...)
➤ other people...   may view us differently (was that the experience of anyone in the previous section?)
                     affect what we want to be like (give examples).

Going deeper...

Level One

The idea is... that the young people will become aware that they are made up of body, mind, emotions *and* spirit.

YOU MAY NEED
A large sheet of
    paper OR a board
    OR an OHP acetate
Suitable pens

1. Introduce this by stating that, although we are very different from each other in many respects, we are all basically made up of the same 4 things...

2. Talk very simply and very briefly about BODY, MIND and EMOTIONS - write each word on a piece of paper, board or OHP acetate if you wish.

3. Talk together about the following, fairly common, experiences:

   ➤ eating a meal
   ➤ listening to your favourite piece of music
   ➤ facing a challenge (in an exam, a sport... and so on) - and succeeding!
   ➤ getting a hug
   ➤ looking at something spectacular in nature (the stars, a fantastic view... and so on)
   ➤ making decisions - move on from everyday decisions to big decisions, those which involve a choice between right and wrong... and so on

   For each one, ask the young people: *which part of us is involved in this - body, mind, emotions...?* Concentrate on raising awareness of how each is more than just a physical experience - eating a meal, for example, obviously involves body as hunger is satisfied, but what about our enjoyment of the tastes? Try also to see whether your young people identify anything else, something which is neither body nor mind nor emotions in any of the above (for example, a sense of awe, an appreciation of beauty, a conscience, values, intuition...)

4. Introduce the idea that we also have a SPIRIT - write this word on the paper, board or OHP acetate if appropriate. Ask the young people:

   ~ *What do you think this means?*
   ~ *Do you think you have a spirit? If so, what part of you is it?*
   [BE VERY CAUTIOUS HERE!! Your young people will be aware of spiritual things from films and TV, and some will also have experimented with ouija boards and the like... our aim here is to raise awareness of the fact that God created us with a spirit in order to have a growing relationship with Him and **not** to foster interest in the occult and paranormal!]

5. Make the following points as appropriate, inviting the young people to respond to what you say:

   ➤ we're not always aware of it, but just as we have a body, a mind and emotions, we all have a spirit...
   ➤ God created us with a spirit so that we could respond to Him
   ➤ our spirits have been deadened by our decision to ignore God and all He wants for our lives
   ➤ only God, through Jesus, can make us alive again in our spirit
   ➤ until this happens, there will always be part of us searching for 'something else'...

6. Encourage the young people to look for 'evidence' of body, mind, emotions and spirit as they go through the week.

   | *End.* |

Level Two

The idea is... that the young people understand how God views them.

YOU WILL NEED

To prepare the words

In advance, photocopy the words on pages 10 and 11 and cut along the dotted lines.

1. Introduce this by mentioning how interested we are in what other people think of us (give examples)... but how aware are we of what God thinks about us?

2. Tack the words 'HE' and 'ME' on the board or wall, about 30cms apart.

3. Cover each of the following areas briefly and simply - as you talk about each one, tack the appropriate word in between 'HE' and 'ME' as a focus point and memory-aid before moving on to the next. The references in brackets will help you as you prepare!

HE knows ME	(Psalm 103:14; Matthew 6:31-32 + 10:30)
HE loves ME	(Psalm 103:11+17; John 3:16; Romans 5:7-8; Ephesians 2:4-5; 1 John 3:1a)
HE cares for ME	(Matthew 6:28-30 + 11:28)
HE saves ME	(Psalm 91:14 + 103:4)
HE forgives ME	(Psalm 103:13; 1 John 1:7+9)
HE protects ME	(Psalm 91:2+5; Isaiah 43:2)
HE values ME	(Psalm 8:5-6)

> **go to FOCUS AND ACT**

Level Three

The idea is... that the young people understand how God views them.

YOU WILL NEED

To make copies
Pens
Bibles

In advance, make photocopies of page 12, enough for one per person.

1. Give everyone a copy of the sheet, a pen and a Bible.

2. Ask the young people to complete the sentences in their own words using the Bible verses - please see the completed sheet on page 13 for guidelines! (Bear in mind that some will be quicker than others - suggest working from the outside in or in small groups, so that everyone gets a flavour of each of the areas)

3. Discuss and reflect on what the group has discovered:

   ~ *Which verses surprise you?*
   ~ *Are there any which you find difficult to believe?*
   ~ *Which one/ones appeal to you most?*

(Possibly draw attention to the significance of the diamond shape... we are **this** precious in God's sight!)

 your group are less comfortable with using a Bible...
Copy the 'diamond' onto a large sheet of paper or OHP slide. Ask individuals to look up a reference each and complete the sentences as a whole group.

Focus and act

1. If possible, have a few moments of quiet... ask the young people to focus particularly on the truth of what God thinks they are like.

2. Point out that there will be differences between our own self-image and God's truth about us:

   we may feel underneath that we are better than lots of other people... but this can't be the case, because the honour, love, care (and so on) which God shows us, He shows to everyone else too!

   OR

   we may feel UNlovely, worthLESS, UNcared for... the Bible tells us very clearly that these are feelings shaped by things in our lives and not true facts... to God, each of us is very, very precious indeed!

3. Ask the young people to try to recognise one or two key differences between their own self-image and God's truth about them.

4. As appropriate to your group, suggest that they:

   ➤ pray about this this week
   ➤ trust that God can and will do something about this... but that it may be a gradual change

   OR

   just say that God loves us very much indeed just as we are, but that He loves us too much to leave us just as we are!

5. Use these guidelines to PRAY for your young people or have a time of PRAYER in small groups...

   ... praise God that we are each unique and precious in His sight
   ... express to Him the things which we find difficult to accept about ourselves
   ... ask to be able to see who we really are and to trust Him with all of ourselves.

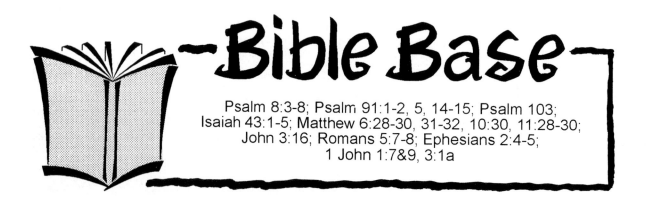

Bible Base

Psalm 8:3-8; Psalm 91:1-2, 5, 14-15; Psalm 103; Isaiah 43:1-5; Matthew 6:28-30, 31-32, 10:30, 11:28-30; John 3:16; Romans 5:7-8; Ephesians 2:4-5; 1 John 1:7&9, 3:1a

How reliable would you say you are?	What would you change about yourself, if you could?	What are you scared of?
Will you spend the rest of your life in this area? If not, why not?	How do you see yourself in 20 years time?	What's your most embarrassing moment?
How would you spend your ideal holiday?	Which is your favourite record?	If you were Prime Minister, what would you do?
Which of your possessions would you least like to lose?	If you were going out for a meal, where would you choose to go?	What influences what you wear?
Which animal is most like you? Why?	What do you read?	What will influence your choice of career? Money? Job satisfaction? Something else?
What are you looking forward to?	Which TV programme/film would you most like to appear in?	If you had more leisure time, what would you do?

Which country would you most like to visit?	Who or what makes you laugh?	What qualities do you look for in a friend?
What is your earliest memory?	When would you tell a lie?	What really annoys you?
Which living person do you most admire?	Do you have an ambition?	What is your idea of a really good night out?
If your mum/dad really disapproved of one of your friends, what would you do?	Describe your ideal partner!	If your friends were going to a night club, but you were under age, what would you do?
What would you do with £10,000?	Why do you come to this group?	When or where were you happiest?
If you saw your best friend's boy/girl-friend out with someone else, what would you do?	What do you feel strongly about?	Would you go on a blind date?

moody

Are you...?

kind

cautious

thoughtful

artistic

STRONG-WILLED

AMBITIOUS

ADVENTUROUS

musical

studious

easily-influenced

HONEST

Athletic

self-confident

happy

shy

HARD-WORKING

patient

LOUD

Trustworthy

Witty

Self-controlled

HE ME

loves

cares for

saves

10

knows

forgives

protects

values

11

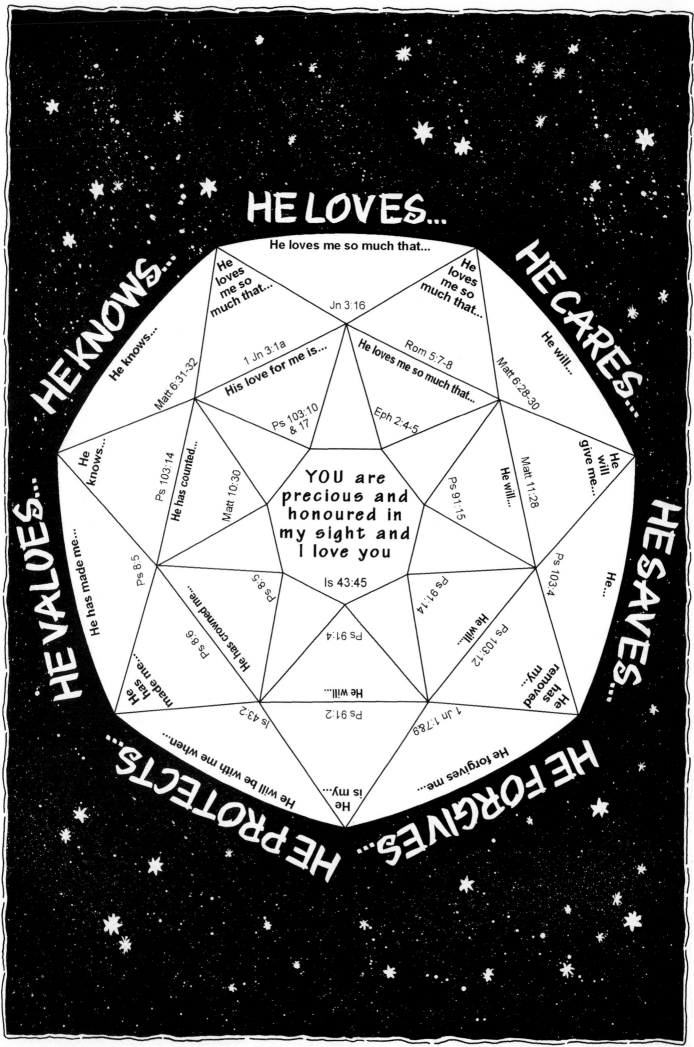

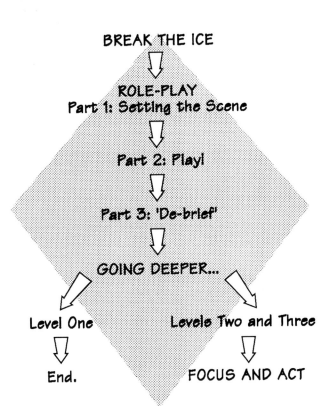

BREAK THE ICE

ROLE-PLAY
Part 1: Setting the Scene

Part 2: Play!

Part 3: 'De-brief'

GOING DEEPER...

Level One   Levels Two and Three

End.   FOCUS AND ACT

We want our young people to...

- learn about our relationship with God from the parable of the prodigal son

- focus on their relationship with God at present

- consider how up-to-date the family situation in the parable is!

2. God and Me

Break the ice

The idea is... that the young people 'warm up' with a drama exercise around the theme of families.

YOU MAY NEED
A camera

1. Ask the young people to get into groups - any number between 3 and 8 would be fine!

2. Each group represents a family - ask each individual to choose any role within a family (aunt, father, step-brother and so on).

3. Read out the following situations one by one - after each one, allow about a minute for the young people to think, move and then freeze still so that they look like a photo:

   ➤ a wedding
   ➤ a holiday
   ➤ Christmas
   ➤ a night in...

   Have each group show their 'photo' before moving on to the next situation -the results might be funny or serious, depending on the personalities of the individuals involved!

4. You may like to actually take some photos and have them on display for the next session!

if **your young people are creative...**
Let them think up their own family situations, form a 'photo' and have the rest of the group try to guess what is going on!

Role-play

> **The idea is...** to really get the young people involved in the prodigal son situation, so that the impact of its message is strong and clear.

DON'T DULL THE IMPACT BY MENTIONING THE PARABLE ITSELF YET!

PART 1: Setting the scene

YOU WILL NEED
To prepare the role outlines

It's important to get these stages right for the role-play to work!

In advance, make copies of the role outlines on page 20, and cut along the dotted lines - you will need one outline per person.

1. Ask the young people to get into groups of 3 (include yourself and other leaders if necessary): within the 3's, ask one person to be 'A', one to be 'B' and one to be 'C' - the role-play will take place in these groups, but for now....

2. ....group all the 'A's' together, all the 'B's' together and all the 'C's' together: we suggest that these groups should not be bigger than 8, so you may need to divide them again!

3. Give the: 'A's' the PARENT role card,
             'B's' the ELDER SON/DAUGHTER role card,
             'C's' the YOUNGER SON/DAUGHTER role card,
   and allow time for the thinking and discussion outlined on each card.

PART 2: Play!

4. Ask the young people to get back into their original groups of 3, staying 'in character' as they do so.

5. Announce the scenes one by one, and allow time for the young people to act out what happens:

   Scene 1 - Evening, after a long day: everything seems normal, until the younger son/daughter arrives and announces his/her decision to leave home...
   (Time guideline - 1 1/2 mins.)

   Scene 2 - The next morning: the younger son/daughter prepares to go, demanding the money he/she feels is rightly his/hers from the family business...
   (Time guideline - 2 mins.)

   Scene 3 - Several months later: the younger son/daughter returns - it is clear that his/her 'adventure' has been a complete disaster...
   (Time guideline - 2 mins.)

6. Perhaps have one or two groups perform their role-plays - ask everyone to show appreciation (of their courage, if not necessarily of their acting ability!)

PART 3: 'De-brief'

7. Talk together about the scenes which have just been role-played, focusing on:

➤ general feelings about the 3 characters
➤ the main issues, eg   ~ **When should parents 'let go'?**
                        ~ **When should you be allowed to make your own**
                          mistakes?
                        ~ **What causes jealousy and tensions in family**
                          relationships?

and any others raised by the young people.

Going deeper...

The idea is... that the young people move on to look at the parable as a picture of our relationship with God.

Level One

YOU WILL NEED
A large piece of paper
   OR a board OR an
   OHP acetate
Suitable pens

1. Begin by pointing out that, although this situation is very up-to-date, it is actually taken from a story told by Jesus.

2. Explain, in your own words, how the father **in Jesus' parable** reacted to his younger son, contrasting this with what happened at the end of the role-plays.

3. State that the story also has a meaning on a deeper level: Jesus went on to explain that the story was really all about God and people...

4. In pairs or small groups, ask the young people to share their ideas about God, along the following lines:

   ~ *Do you believe in God? Can you say why/why not?*
   ~ *If there is a God, what is He like?*

5. Gather the whole group together again, ask for feedback from the small groups and let the discussion run...- write the main points and ideas up on the paper, board or OHP.

6. Summarise the characteristics your young people believe God has - go back to the parable and talk about the father's characteristics... then state that Jesus told the story to help us understand that **this** is what God is like!

7. Ask the young people to react to the father character as a picture of God **(- are they surprised by it? What are the differences with their own image of God?)**

8. Sum up and end the session.

End.

Levels Two and Three

YOU MAY NEED

To rehearse the reading!

1. Begin by pointing out that, although this situation is very up-to-date, it is actually taken from a story told by Jesus. (If appropriate to your group, really stress this: perhaps the Bible might have something to say to us in the 1990's after all!)

2. **EITHER** role-read the parable **OR** read it straight from **Luke 15:11-32**.

3. State that Jesus used this parable to explain what our relationship with God is and can be like.

4. Work through the following points, as appropriate to your young people:

THE FATHER

a) Ask: ***how did the 'parents' react in the last scene of the role-plays?*** Draw out the following possibilities:

➤ anger
➤ 'the cold shoulder'
➤ an inquisition about what actually happened... (to the money?)
➤ constant references to failure, letting the family down...
➤ a very guarded welcome (plus "I told you so" or "serves you right")

b) Ask: ***how does this contrast with the reactions of the father in the parable?***
Bring out the following points:

➤ he was absolutely overjoyed to see his son return home
➤ he was not angry or accusing
➤ he did not impose conditions ("I'll have you back only when.....")

c) "Jesus is explaining that this is how God reacts to anyone who turns back to Him!"

THE YOUNGER SON/DAUGHTER

a) "In many ways we are like him/her, because we have turned our backs on God and wanted to go our own way."

b) Ask: ***who could identify with this character in the role-play?*** Emphasise the attractions of leaving home and gaining independence in the role-play situation...

c) "Just like this, many of the things we do, which are turning our back on God, seem attractive or just plain normal!"

d) Ask for examples of this and be ready with your own suggestions (eg we can't see anything wrong with how we act in a particular personal relationship, with what we do with our time, with what we do with our lives...) If appropriate, state clearly that it is possible to be a Christian, but still be acting like the youngest in particular areas of our lives.

e) "Jesus is showing us that if we are choosing to go our own way rather than God's way, then we have broken the relationship with Him - this will have consequences..!"

f) Remind your group of the father's reaction to his son when he came to his senses and returned home...

g) "This is the welcome which awaits us when we face up to where we have gone wrong and turn back to God!"

THE ELDER SON/DAUGHTER

a) "Jesus used this character to criticise the attitudes of some 'religious' people, who were in many ways jealous of Christians and refused to accept them..."

b) "If we have been a Christian for a long time or come from a church background, we can sometimes fall into the same trap of a less-than-welcoming attitude towards new Christians - could this be you?"

Focus and act

YOU WILL NEED
To make copies
Pens

In advance, make copies of the 'cartoon' sheet on page 21, enough for one per person.

1. Give everyone a copy of the sheet and a pen.

2. Reminding the group that the parable is really about our relationship with God, ask the young people to look at the 'cartoon' and think about where they are on it - they should circle the picture which represents them at the moment (it's possible to circle more than one. or to add another figure).

3. Lead into a time of PRAYER - remind the young people about the son's attitude as he returned to his father, pointing out that we shouldn't, therefore, just breeze into God's presence...

   .... thank God for the incredible welcome which awaits us when we turn back to Him
   .... allow space for individuals to acknowledge their position before Him, and to respond as appropriate (- you may well need to offer guidance and advice on a one-to-one basis here)

Luke 15:11-32

Role-play

parent

You are a parent of two young adults, running a family business together. Your eldest works long hours and shares your wish to keep really close family ties. Your youngest, however, seems restless...

▶ **What are you like as a person? (use your imagination!)**
▶ **What are your interests, priorities, worries...?**
▶ **How do you react to the others in your family?**

Role-play

elder son/daughter

You are the elder of the two - the family business, still run by your mother/father, offers a secure future. You work long hours, are keen to keep really close family ties and would consider yourself to be loyal and reliable: the same could certainly not be said of your younger brother/sister...

▶ **What are you like as a person? (use your imagination!)**
▶ **What are your interests, priorities, worries...?**
▶ **How do you react to the others in your family?**

Role-play

younger son/daughter

You are the younger of two - the family business, still run by your mother/father, offers a secure future. Your elder brother/sister is happy to settle for this, but you are feeling restless: you are sure that there is more to life...

▶ **What are you like as a person? (use your imagination!)**
▶ **What are your interests, priorities, worries...?**
▶ **How do you react to the others in your family?**

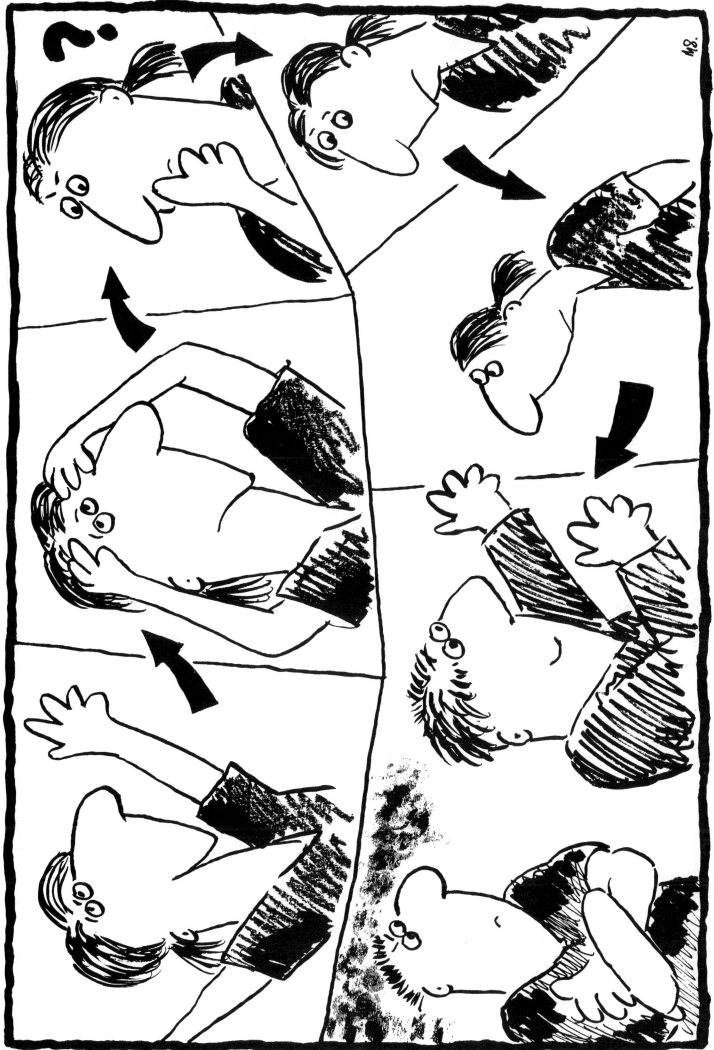

21

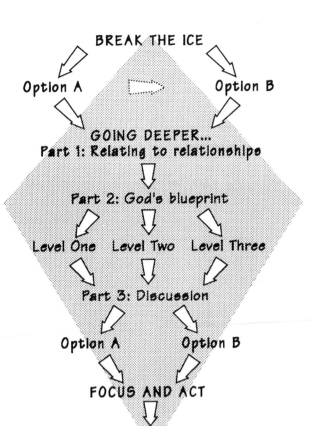

BREAK THE ICE

Option A   Option B

GOING DEEPER...
Part 1: Relating to relationships

Part 2: God's blueprint

Level One   Level Two   Level Three

Part 3: Discussion

Option A   Option B

FOCUS AND ACT

DRAMA: THE MAKER'S INSTRUCTIONS

We want our young people to...

- become more aware of the different relationships in their lives

- identify God's 'blueprint' for relationships

- see the need to live by the 'Maker's instructions' if relationships are going to work.

3. God, Me and Others

Break the ice

The idea is... using one of two games, to encourage the young people to think about the different relationships they are in and about the stereotyped behaviour we expect in these relationships.

Choose the activity or activities which would work best with your group!

Option A: Party guests

YOU WILL NEED
To prepare the party roles

(Bear in mind... not eveyone will want to play this!)

In advance, prepare small slips of paper, each with a relationship written on it (eg mother, father, neighbour, teacher, younger brother/sister, employer, great aunt... and so on).

1. Choose someone to play the 'host' - he/she should be good at acting spontaneously and preferably also someone you have been able to brief in advance!

2. Give out one slip of paper to several young people, asking them not to show anyone else at this stage.

3. Explain that the young people are to arrive at the party acting towards the 'host' according to the character on their slip of paper.

4. Have the guests arrive one by one - the rest of the group have to guess what the relationship is between the 'host' and the guest!

Option B: Just a minute

YOU WILL NEED

To prepare the playing cards
An accurate (and preferably visible) minute timer

In advance, prepare a set of 8 cards, each with a different relationship written on it - have as broad a range as possible!

1. Establish 2 teams of 2 players each.

2. Taking each team in turn, pick up a card and read out the relationship written on it - one young person has to speak for one minute about this relationship without hesitation, deviation or repitition.

3. The young person may be challenged by anyone else in the group - if the challenge is upheld, the subject passes to his/her team-mate and then on to the other team.

4. The team which is speaking when the minute is up wins the round!

 your young people are less confident and outgoing...
Reduce the speaking time to 30 seconds

OR

 you would prefer to involve the whole group...
Read out one card and ask the first young person to begin speaking about that relationship - move on to the next person when there is a successful challenge and start a new topic after one minute.

Going deeper...

The idea is... to show that the Bible is relevant to this area of our lives and to highlight the things which God tells us make good relationships - and those which break them too!

PART 1

YOU WILL NEED

To prepare the outline
A thick, bold pen

In advance, copy the outline on page 29 onto a large (approximately A2 size) piece of paper.

1. Tack up the outline on a board or wall.

2. Ask for a volunteer to write for the group.

3. Ask the whole group: *what relationships do we have?* Have the volunteer write all the suggestions on the top part of the sheet as they are made -encourage your young people to think in broad terms (please see the completed sheet on page 30 for guidelines!)

4. As soon as you have a good selection, move on to...

PART 2: God's blueprint
Level One

YOU WILL NEED
To make sets of 'cards'

<u>In advance, make copies of page 31</u> and cut along the dotted lines to form separate 'cards' - you will need one set for every 3 or 4 young people.

1. Ask the young people to get into groups of 3 or 4.

2. Ask them to 'brainstorm' the kinds of things which BUILD relationships... and those which BREAK relationships.

3. Explain that you are going to look together at what the Bible has to say about what BUILDS and what BREAKS relationships, and hand out a set of 'cards' to each group.

4. In the small groups, ask the young people to:

   ➤ see which things they had already identified in the 'brainstorm',
   ➤ separate the 'builders' from the 'breakers',
   ➤ talk about which of the 'builders' are most important (perhaps trying to put them in some kind of order)... and then which of the 'breakers' are most destructive.

5. Bring the group back together again and ask for some feedback - as the 'builders' and 'breakers' are mentioned, write them up on the large outline (please see page 30 again for guidelines)

6. Sum up:

   ➤ highlighting the key relationship 'builders', and explain that you will go on to look at these in future sessions...
   ➤ stressing the point that these 'builders' and 'breakers' all came from God's 'blueprint' for relationships in the Bible - a challenge to the view that the Bible is out of date and irrelevant!!

| *go to Part 3* |

Level Two

YOU WILL NEED
To make copies

<u>In advance, make copies of the passages on pages 32 and 33</u>, enough for one for every 6 to 8 young people.

1. Ask the young people to get into groups of 3 or 4.

2. Give half the groups one copy of the Colossians passage and the rest of the groups one copy of the Ephesians passage. Now give them 10 minutes to look for answers to the question: *from what God says to us through these verses, what BUILDS and what BREAKS relationships?*

| *go to Level Three, point 4* |

Level Three

In advance, make copies of the outline on page 29, enough for one per person, as a memory aid from this session.

1. Ask the young people to get into groups of 3 or 4.

2. Give out the outlines, Bibles and pens, as appropriate.

3. Ask half of the groups to look up **Colossians 3:8-14** and the other half to look up **Ephesians 4:25-32 + 5:1-2.** Now give them 10 minutes to look for answers to the question: *from what God says to us through these verses, what BUILDS and what BREAKS relationships?*

4. Bringing the whole group together again, complete the outline:

   EITHER have a spokesperson from each group report back on what has been discovered, with the volunteer 'scribe' writing on the large outline,

   OR ask someone from each group to write answers on the large outline as they discover them during the group time.

   Write the things which BUILD relationships along the brick shapes and the things which BREAK (or undermine) relationships underneath, as on the completed outline on page 30.

5. Sum up, talking very briefly about any words and phrases which you think need a little explanation, and highlighting the key 'ingredients' - point out that these will be the subject of future sessions.

PART 3: Discussion

Choose the activity or activities which would work best with your group!

Option A: 'Confidential'

YOU WILL NEED
To make copies

In advance, make copies of the problem page letters on page 34, enough for one for every 2 to 3 young people.

1. Ask the young people to find a partner or form a group of 3.

2. Give a copy of the problem page letters to each pair or threesome.

3. Ask the young people to look at the situations and, work out which 'building blocks' (trust, honesty, kindness) are missing and which 'breakers' (selfishness, malice) need to be dealt with!

4. Ask for feedback - the situations are reasonably complex, so bring out things which may have been overlooked (eg 'righteous' anger in the step-brother scenario...but revenge would not be justified!)

5. Open up the discussion, focussing on how God's instructions are helpful and relevant in all our relationships!

Option B: Open discussion

1. Guide the group in discussion with the following questions:

   ~ *God has given us clear guidelines about the things which make or break relationships - do you agree with them?*
   ~ *Do these guidelines apply to some relationships more than others?*
   ~ *From your experience, when have you seen these guidelines helping to build a relationship?*

2. Bring out clearly that God's instructions are very relevant, helpful and that they apply to ALL our relationships!

Focus and act

1. **EITHER** focus on a relationship:

   Ask each young person to think of one relationship they have been troubled by - can they identify what has gone wrong according to these guidelines? Suggest they think about it during the week to try to finish the statement: "I think my relationship with.......... has been difficult because...................."

   OR focus on a theme:

   Take a theme (eg anger, dishonesty, unhelpful talk) and ask the young people to think about it during the week, trying to finish the statement: "Anger (or whatever theme you choose) has affected my relationship with.......... because...................."

2. Remind the group that there will be sessions later on to help them put relationships right when things have gone wrong!

3. Use these guidelines to PRAY for your young people or have a short time of PRAYER in small groups...

   ... thank God that He has left us clear and helpful instructions about relationships in the Bible
   ... ask for God's help to identify where relationships are going wrong and to begin to put things right...

Drama: 'The maker's instructions'

The idea is... to finish with a light-hearted sketch, making the point that everything goes better when we follow the maker's instructions...

YOU WILL NEED
To rehearse the sketch

<u>In advance, allocate parts for the sketch on pages 35 and 36</u> and arrange a time to run through it.

Perform the drama - it speaks for itself and probably needs no comment!

FOR THE NEXT SESSION...

You will need a short video clip from a TV Drama or 'Soap'

Ask the young people to bring along some magazines

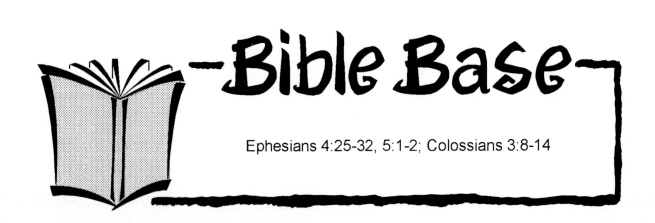

Bible Base

Ephesians 4:25-32, 5:1-2; Colossians 3:8-14

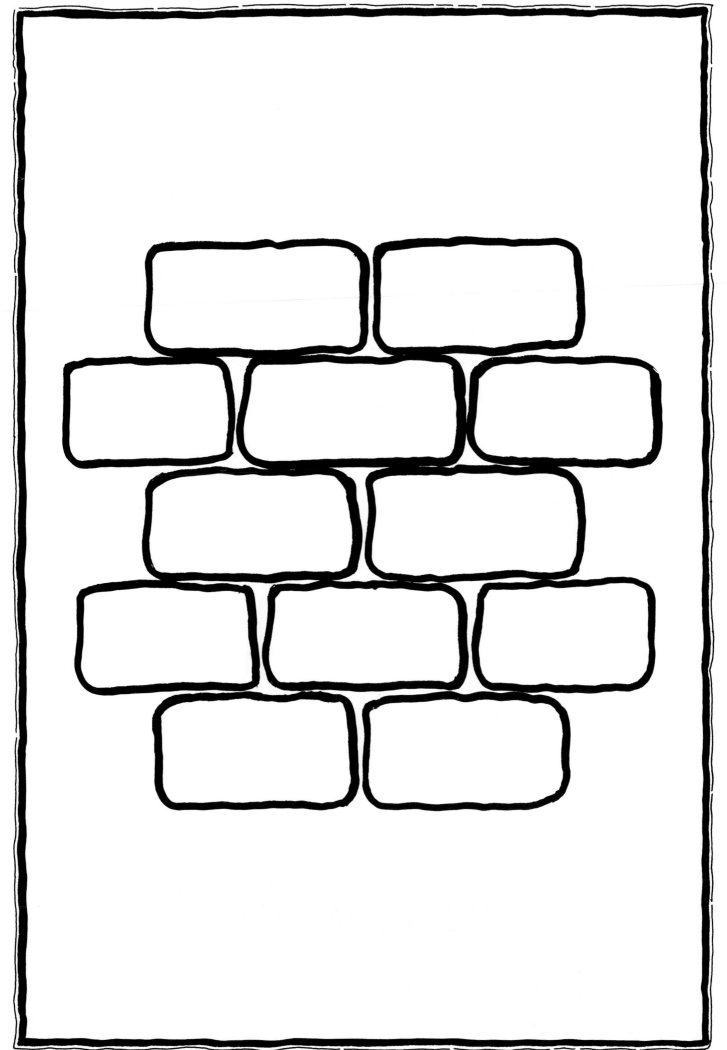

STEP-BROTHER/SISTER   SON/DAUGHTER   EMPLOYEE
YOUTH GROUP MEMBER   AUNT/UNCLE   CITIZEN
TEAM - MEMBER   BROTHER/SISTER   NEIGHBOUR
NIECE/NEPHEW   FRIEND   COUSIN
BOY/GIRLFRIEND   PARENT   COLLEAGUE
CLASS-MATE   PUPIL

COMPASSION
(COL 3:12)

KINDNESS
(COL 3:12 + EPH 4:32)

HUMILITY
(COL 3:12)

GENTLENESS
(COL 3:12)

NEW LIFE, NEW SELF
(COL 3:10)

PATIENCE
(COL 3:12)

TOLERANCE
(COL 3:13)

FORGIVENESS
(COL 3:13 + EPH 4:32)

LOVE
(COL 3:14)

HONESTY
(EPH 4:25)

HELPFUL WORDS
(EPH 4:29)

TENDER-HEARTEDNESS
(EPH 4:32)

LIES (COL 3:9 + EPH 4:25)

ANGER (COL 3:8 + EPH 4:26)

PREJUDICE (COL 3:11)

HARMFUL WORDS (EPH 4:29)

HATEFUL FEELINGS (COL 3:8 + EPH 4:31)

PASSION (COL 3:8)

OBSCENE TALK (COL 3:8)

SHOUTING (EPH 4:31)

INSULTS (COL 3:8)

BITTERNESS (EPH 4:31)

lying	honesty	kindness
holding a grudge	insults	patience
meanness	anger	quarrelling
bitterness	gentleness	hatred
humility	intolerance	love
forgiveness	saying things which build others up...	always putting yourself first

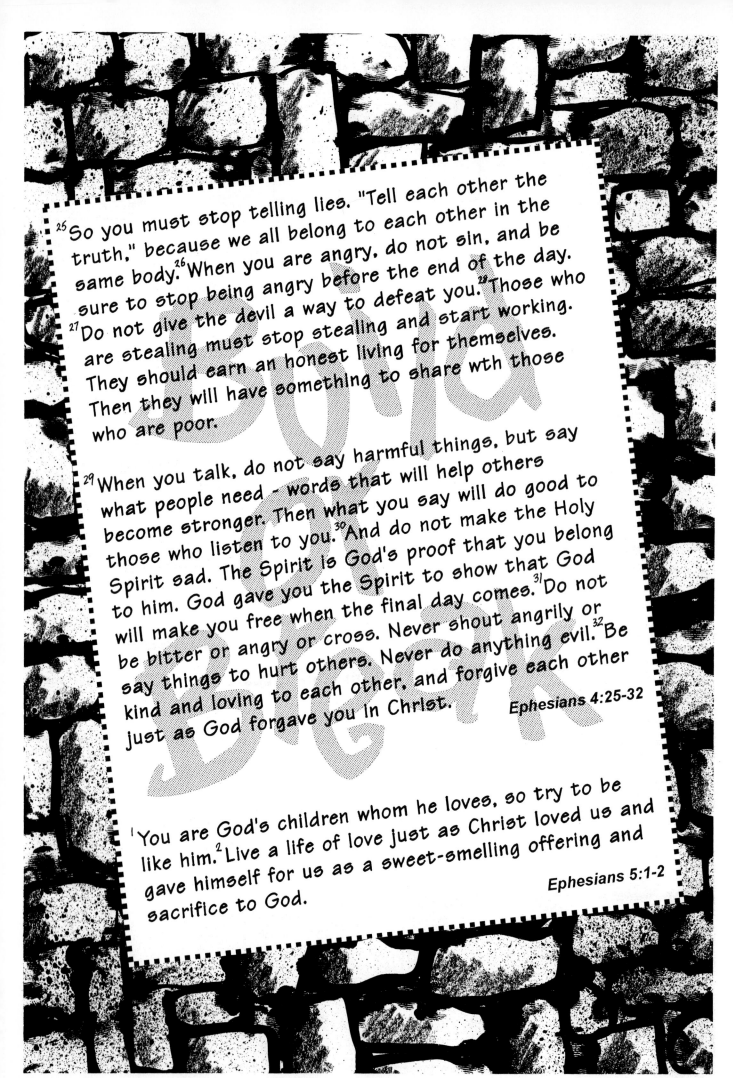

²⁵So you must stop telling lies. "Tell each other the truth," because we all belong to each other in the same body.²⁶When you are angry, do not sin, and be sure to stop being angry before the end of the day. ²⁷Do not give the devil a way to defeat you.²⁸Those who are stealing must stop stealing and start working. They should earn an honest living for themselves. Then they will have something to share wth those who are poor.

²⁹When you talk, do not say harmful things, but say what people need - words that will help others become stronger. Then what you say will do good to those who listen to you.³⁰And do not make the Holy Spirit sad. The Spirit is God's proof that you belong to him. God gave you the Spirit to show that God will make you free when the final day comes.³¹Do not be bitter or angry or cross. Never shout angrily or say things to hurt others. Never do anything evil.³²Be kind and loving to each other, and forgive each other just as God forgave you in Christ.

Ephesians 4:25-32

¹You are God's children whom he loves, so try to be like him.²Live a life of love just as Christ loved us and gave himself for us as a sweet-smelling offering and sacrifice to God.

Ephesians 5:1-2

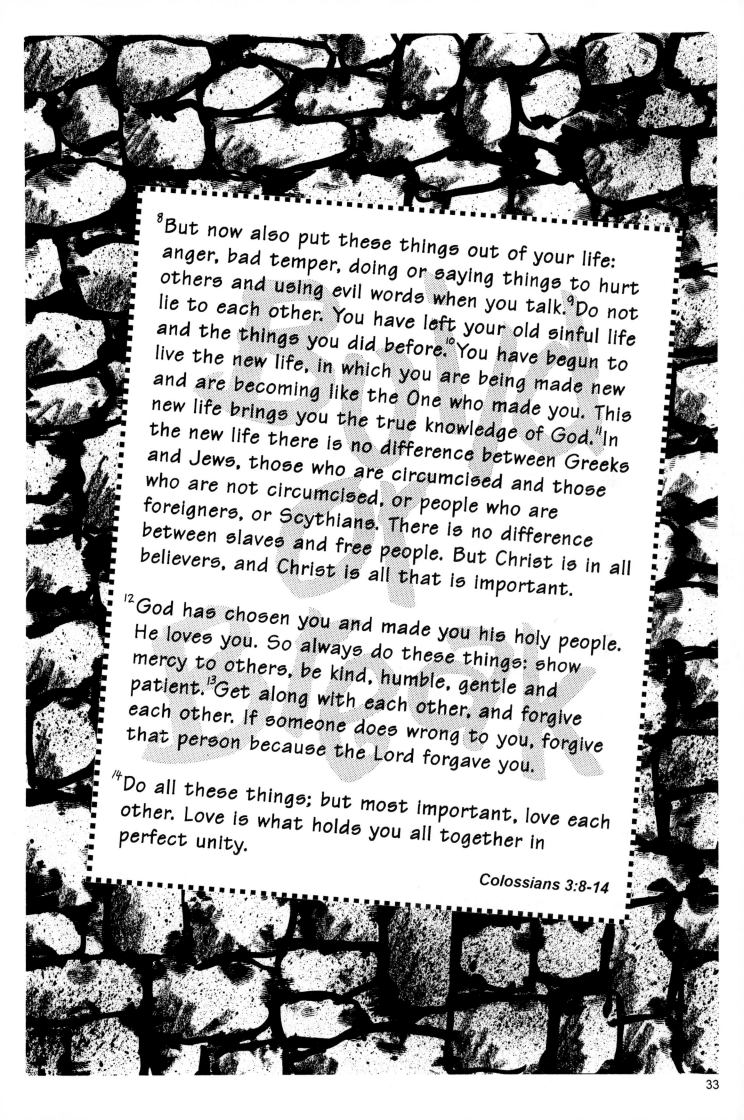

8But now also put these things out of your life: anger, bad temper, doing or saying things to hurt others and using evil words when you talk. 9Do not lie to each other. You have left your old sinful life and the things you did before. 10You have begun to live the new life, in which you are being made new and are becoming like the One who made you. This new life brings you the true knowledge of God. 11In the new life there is no difference between Greeks and Jews, those who are circumcised and those who are not circumcised, or people who are foreigners, or Scythians. There is no difference between slaves and free people. But Christ is in all believers, and Christ is all that is important.

12God has chosen you and made you his holy people. He loves you. So always do these things: show mercy to others, be kind, humble, gentle and patient. 13Get along with each other, and forgive each other. If someone does wrong to you, forgive that person because the Lord forgave you.

14Do all these things; but most important, love each other. Love is what holds you all together in perfect unity.

Colossians 3:8-14

SHE'S BEING SO BORING!

My friend is really getting on my nerves. Her parents have split up recently, but anybody would think it was the end of the world! She doesn't want to go out and says she just wants quiet nights in and someone to talk to. I'm seriously thinking of finding some other friends if she doesn't stop being so boring...

MY GIRLFRIEND IS EMBARRASSING ME

I've been going out with this girl for three months now and although I really like her, she's starting to make me look stupid in front of other people, going on about what I'm wearing or about something I've said. It's making me miserable. I've tried talking to her about it, but she says she's only joking and laughs it off...

I'M BULLIED BY MY STEP-BROTHER

I can't stand my step-brother. He's always been really nasty to me, taking my stuff without asking, thumping me when no-one is looking, getting me into trouble with mum, teachers and so on. You'd think he would grow out of it, but he seems to be getting worse. I can't take it any more. I can't hit him back and he knows it, but I've thought of loads of other ways of getting him back...

MY PARENTS TREAT ME AS IF I'M A CHILD

Everybody I know has parents who are under-standing, but mine are so unreasonable! I mean, I'm old enough to decide for myself, but they still want to know what I'm doing the whole time - it's none of their business! I've started to be a bit more careful about what I say about where I'm going or who I'm going with - it's not lying exactly, it's just not quite telling the truth, like last Saturday, for example...

34

Life is like a deckchair

Characters: **A** & **B** - Narrators
                  C, D & **E** - Actors

Props: Deckchair
             Lightbulb
             A book

A: Ladies and Gentlemen, Life
     [*Enter* C *in attitude of Rodin's thinker.*]
B: Is like
A: A deckchair.
     [*Enter* D *with deckchair -* C *looks put out.*]
B: Well, fairly like a deckchair.
     [D *looks put out,* C *begins to smile.*]
A: There is some *slight* resemblance.
     [C *makes gesture to* D *to get off stage,* D *exits with deckchair in a
     huff.*]
B: Or to put another way, we tried to think of a sketch that was
     profound.
     [C *makes appropriate gestures.*]
A: Searching.
B: Meaningful.
A: And which explains why *we* follow Jesus.
B: And so after much agonised thought
A: We came up with a little sketch entitled
B: Life
A: Is like
B: A lampost.
     [C *takes out lamp bulb and assumes position of lampost.*]
A: This however led to certain
B: Unforeseen problems.
     [*Enter* D *as dog which goes up to lampost...*]
D: Wooff, wooff!
C: Get off, get off!! Cut it out.
     [*Exit lampost pursued by dog -* C & D.]
A: So instead we concluded that life is like
B   The aforementioned
     [D *enters with deckchair.*]
A: Deckchair
B: A deckchair promises happiness, contentment and fulfilment, but
     contains certain hidden complexities and unforeseen difficulties in
     which respect it is, as you will agree

A: Rather like life.

B: Some people approach the putting up of a deckchair full of confidence in their own abilities. They ignore the maker's instructions

A: Pull the bar at the bottom

B: Extend the bar at the top. And then...

A: Collapse in a heap on the floor.
[D *collapses, struck by deckchair and lies motionless*]
[*Enter* C *with book.*]

B: Others are more careful in their approach. They begin by reading the maker's instructions, but fail to act on them. And succeed in producing something that looks like a deckchair

A: But isn't
[*Deckchair collapses and* C *rolls on the floor and lies motionless.*]

B: There are some however who read the maker's instructions
[*Enter* E *with book.*]

A: Follow the maker's advice

B: And succeed in producing a firm

A: Steady

B: And reliable

A: Deckchair
[E *sits down in chair.*]

B: Which leads us as you will have realised

A: To the moral.

B: The moral: Life has a slight

A: Very slight

B: Resemblance to a deckchair.

A: But life is *much* more complicated.

B: So how can *we* expect to put our lives together

A: Without consulting the maker's instructions?

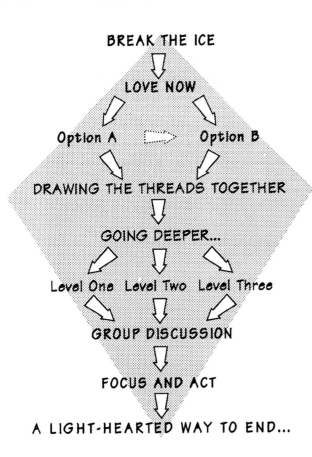

BREAK THE ICE
⬇
LOVE NOW
↙ ↘
Option A ⇨ Option B
⬇ ⬇
DRAWING THE THREADS TOGETHER
⬇
GOING DEEPER...
↙ ⬇ ↘
Level One Level Two Level Three
↘ ⬇ ↙
GROUP DISCUSSION
⬇
FOCUS AND ACT
⬇
A LIGHT-HEARTED WAY TO END...

We want our young people to...

■ consider how society views love

■ reflect on what they themselves think love is

■ understand what God means by love

■ be clear about how much God loves them and how they can love Him in return

■ learn who, how and why we should love, according to the Bible.

4. What is Love?

To set the scene

Have soft lights or candles and play soft, romantic music to create an atmosphere as your young people arrive....

Break the ice

YOU WILL NEED
To record a short video clip
A TV and video player

In advance, video an episode of a TV drama or 'soap' and select a 5-minute clip, showing several relationships in which love is supposed to exist.

1. Play the clip, asking the young people to look out for:

   ➤ who loves whom,
   ➤ what kind of love this is,
   ➤ how true to life it is.

2. Have a very brief discussion around the answers to these questions.

Love now

The idea is... that the young people become more aware of how love is viewed in society and reflect on their own perception of love.

Choose the activity or activities which would best suit your group!

Option A: Images

YOU WILL NEED

To make a collection
A large piece of
    paper OR board
Glue
Scissors
Paints, pencils,
    spray paints,
    pens etc

In advance, collect together magazines, newspapers, greetings cards, song lyrics, cheap romantic paperbacks, and anything else which may provide clues to what people think about love today.... if you remembered to mention this last session, your young people may have brought some things to add, (but don't count on it!)

1. **EITHER** altogether **OR** in smaller groups, ask the young people to create a 'poster' showing love in the 1990's - they can cut out images and phrases and add ideas of their own - encourage them to take a broad view of the word...

2. Talk about the results:

   ➤ ask the young people to pick out something from the 'poster', and to say whether or not they agree with it... and why
   ➤ ask: *is love always positive? Does one kind of love feature more strongly than any other?*

3. Briefly sum up what the young people have said.

Option B: Love poem

YOU WILL NEED
Paper
Pens

1. Give everyone a piece of paper and a pen.

2. Ask them to write the word LOVE downwards on their piece of paper, and then write a poem with the letter L somewhere in the first line, the letter O somewhere in the second...and so on - the poems can be funny or serious!

3. Have the young people read out their poems in groups and talk about the ideas behind them.

Drawing the threads together

The idea is... to summarise this part of the material by 'brainstorming' what love means today.

YOU WILL NEED

A large piece of
    paper OR board
A thick, bold pen
Blu-tack

1. In the centre of a large piece of paper or board, write LOVE in a heart shape.

2. Ask the young people to just shout out any words and phrases which come into their heads, and write them all around the heart as they do so.

➡

YOU WILL NEED
Several large pieces
of paper
Thick, bold pens
Blu-tack

3. Leave this on display for the rest of the session.

 you have a large group...
Divide the young people into groups of 5 or 6 and give each group a large piece of paper and a thick, bold pen. 'Brainstorm' the word LOVE as described above. Have each group tack its sheet somewhere around your meeting room and allow 2 or 3 minutes for everyone to mill around and read them.

Going deeper...

The idea is... that the young people will find out for themselves what the Bible has to say about what love is and, as appropriate, about God's love for us and about who, how and why we should love.

Level One

YOU WILL NEED
To prepare a poster
summary
To make copies
Coloured pens
Blu-tack

In advance, make a poster summary of the main points about love from the 1 Corinthians 13 passage: write the word LOVE in large letters in the centre of a large piece of paper (or cut out the individual letters from coloured paper and stick them on.) Also, cut out 17 hearts (each measuring about 12 cms across) from pink or red paper - write one point about love from the passage on each heart ('is patient', 'always hopes'... and so on) and stick them around the word LOVE. Finally, make copies of the passage from page 43, enough for one between two.

1. Ask the young people to find a partner or form a group of 3.

2. Give a copy of the passage and a coloured pen to each pair or threesome.

3. Ask the young people to read through the passage and use the coloured pens to mark it - they might tick or underline things they agree with (two or more ticks or underlines to add emphasis!), put a question mark when they find something they are unsure about, and a cross if there is anything they disagree with...

4. Now ask each pair (or threesome) to join up with another pair (or threesome!) and talk together about what they have marked in the passage.

5. Display your poster summary.

| go to GROUP DISCUSSION |

Level Two

YOU WILL NEED
To cut out heart
outlines
To make copies
A large piece of
paper OR board
Thick, coloured pens
Blu-tack

In advance, cut out about 40 hearts from pink and/or red paper - each heart should measure about 12 cms across. Also, write the word LOVE in large letters in the centre of a large piece of paper or board (or cut out the individual letters from coloured paper and tack them up.) Finally make copies of the verses on pages 44, 45 and 46 - think how many young people you are expecting at your session, divide this number by 3, and make that many copies of *each* passage!

1. Ask the young people to get into 3 groups - we suggest that you split these groups if they contain more than 6 to 8 young people.

2. Give each group 1/3 of the cut-out hearts and a pen.

3. Give: group 1 copies of 'What the Bible says about love',
group 2 copies of 'Who, how and why we love',
group 3 copies of 'How God loves us'.

go to Level Three, point 3

Level Three

YOU WILL NEED
To cut out heart
  outlines
To prepare the Bible
  references
A large piece of
  paper OR board
Thick, coloured pens
Blu-tack

In advance, cut out about 45 hearts from pink and/or red paper - each heart should measure about 12 cms across. Also, write the word LOVE in large letters in the centre of a large piece of paper or board (or cut out the individual letters from coloured paper and tack them up.) Finally, write key Bible references on this theme on some of the heart outlines - you will need one for every 3 to 4 young people, so break up longer passages and/or add others! Suggestions:

  Jesus' teaching on love - Mark 12:28-31, John 13:34-35, Luke 6:27-32
  The more excellent way - 1 Corinthians 13
  God's love and ours - 1 John 4:7-21

1. Ask the young people to get into small groups.

2. Give each group a passage to study, some heart outlines and a pen.

3. Ask the young people to read the verses carefully - as they find a key point about love ask them to write it on a heart outline (one word or phrase per outline), then tack it around the word LOVE on the board or paper.

4. Have an opportunity for the young people to learn what the other groups have discovered,

  EITHER by asking a spokesperson from each small group to report back briefly to the whole group,

  OR, more informally, by inviting everyone to 'mill around' the board or poster and read what has been written in the hearts.

Group discussion

The idea is... to contrast current views about love with what the Bible teaches.

1. Bring the whole group together again, with both the 'brainstorm' sheet and the sheet showing the main points from the Bible study clearly visible.

2. Referring to the points from the Bible study, ask: **what strikes you most and why?** Open up the discussion.

3. Ask: **how are God's ideas about love different from the ones we came up with?** Draw out the following comparisons as appropriate:
[You may wish to begin by explaining briefly that in the Bible there are several words for LOVE - agape, eros, phileo... this will help the young people appreciate that when we say we love something or someone, we actually mean lots of different things!]

(by the way... the idea behind the soft lights, romantic music and all those paper hearts is to really emphasise these contrasts!!)

OUR VIEW....

➤ we tend to emphasise romantic love
➤ we stress feeling

➤ we love a select group of people

➤ love doesn't always last - you can fall in and out of love...
➤ we tend to concentrate on what we can get out of love, not on what we can **give**

➤ love is nice...

GOD'S VIEW....

➤ God is interested in many kinds of love
➤ the Bible also talks about a decision ('all your mind') and choosing to love even when we don't feel like it
➤ God loves everyone, and commands and enables us to do the same
➤ love is eternal

➤ God's love is unconditional - not I LOVE YOU IF.... not I LOVE YOU BECAUSE.... but I LOVE YOU FULL STOP.
➤ love is sometimes costly and often **tough!**

Focus and act

1. Challenge the young people to think of their own 'action plans' for the coming week - offer suggestions appropriate to your young people, such as:

   Are you going to continue looking out for love around you in what you read/ watch/hear, trying to see where it is different from God's ideas?

   Are you going to think carefully about how you love other people? Will you ask for God's help to love with more patience, or more kindness, or less envy, or less pride, or....

   Are you going to think carefully about who you love? Will you try with God's help to love someone whom it's difficult to love?

   Are you aware of how much God loves you? Are you going to think more about how you can love Him in the way you live? (This 'trips up' most Christians at some stage!)

2. Use these guidelines to PRAY for your young people or have a time of PRAYER in small groups...

   ... thank God for His incredible love for each one of us
   ... be honest with Him about the people we find difficult (or impossible!) to love
   ... ask for the Holy Spirit's power to love more as God ask us to...

A light-hearted way to end...

.... Based on what the young people have learnt about God's view of love, go back to the video clip you showed at the beginning - can your young people advise any of the characters..?

FOR THE NEXT SESSION...

Ask 4 or 5 young people to bring in a tape of a song about romantic or sexual love and to write out on a large piece of paper some of the verses and the chorus.

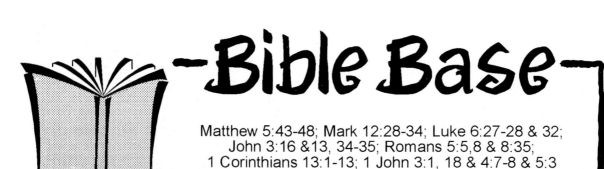

Bible Base

Matthew 5:43-48; Mark 12:28-34; Luke 6:27-28 & 32;
John 3:16 &13, 34-35; Romans 5:5,8 & 8:35;
1 Corinthians 13:1-13; 1 John 3:1, 18 & 4:7-8 & 5:3

What the Bible

LOVE is patient and kind. LOVE is not jealous, it does not boast, and it is not proud. LOVE is not rude, is not selfish, and does not get upset with others. LOVE does not count up wrongs that have been done. LOVE is not happy with evil but is happy with the truth.

LOVE patiently accepts all things. It always trusts, always hopes, and always remains strong. So these three things continue for ever: faith, hope and LOVE. And the greatest of these is LOVE.

...1 Corinthians 13:4-8 & 13...

says about LOVE...

What the Bible

I may speak in different languages of people or even angels. But if I do not have *LOVE* I am only a noisy bell or a crashing cymbal. I may have the gift of prophecy. I may understand all the secret things of God and have all knowledge, and I may have faith so great I can move mountains. But even with all these things, if I do not have *LOVE*, then I am nothing. I may give away everything I have, and I may even give my body as an offering to be burnt. But I gain nothing if I do not have *LOVE*. *LOVE* is patient and kind. *LOVE* is not jealous, it does not boast, and it is not proud. *LOVE* is not rude, is not selfish, and does not get upset with others. *LOVE* does not count up wrongs that have been done. *LOVE* is not happy with evil but is happy with the truth. *LOVE* patiently accepts all things. It always trusts, always hopes, and always remains strong. So these three things continue forever: faith, hope and *LOVE*. And the greatest of these is *LOVE*

...1 Corinthians 13:1-8

& 13...

says about LOVE...

Who, how and

"Which of the commands is most important?" Jesus answered, "The most important command is this: 'Listen, people of Israel! The Lord our God is the only Lord. *LOVE* the Lord your God with all your heart, all your soul, all your mind and all your strength.' The second command is this: '*LOVE* your neighbour as you *LOVE* yourself.' There are no commands more important than these." ...Mark 12:28-31... "I give you a new command: *LOVE* each other. You must *LOVE* each other as I have *LOVED* you. All people will know that you are my followers if you *LOVE* each other." ...John 13:34-35... "But I say to you who are listening, *LOVE* your enemies. Do good to those who hate you, bless those who curse you, pray for those who are cruel to you. If you *LOVE* only the people who *LOVE* you, what praise should you get? Even sinners *LOVE* the people who *LOVE* them." ...Luke 6:27-28 & 32... My children, we should *LOVE* people not only with words and talk, but by our actions and true caring. ...1 John 3:18... Dear friends, we should *LOVE* each other, because *LOVE* comes from God. Everyone who *LOVES* has become God's child and knows God. Whoever does not *LOVE* does not know God, because God is *LOVE*. ...1 John 4:7-8... *LOVING* God means obeying his commands. ...1 John 5:3...

why we LOVE...

45

HOW God

"God **LOVED** the world so much that he gave his one and only Son so that whoever believes in him may not be lost, but have eternal life". ...John 3:16... But God shows his great **LOVE** for us in this way: Christ died for us while we were still sinners. ...Romans 5:8... God has poured out his **LOVE** to fill our hearts. He gave us his **LOVE** through the Holy Spirit. ...Romans 5:5... The Father has **LOVED** us so much that we are called children of God. And we really are his children. ...1 John 3:1... Can anything separate us from the **LOVE** Christ has for us? Can troubles or problems or sufferings or hunger or nakedness or danger or violent death? But in all these things we have full victory through God who showed his **LOVE** for us. Yes, I am sure that neither death, nor life, nor angels, nor ruling spirits, nothing now, nothing in the future, nor powers, nothing above us, nothing below us, nor anything else in the whole world will ever be able to separate us from the **LOVE** of God that is in Christ Jesus our Lord. ...Romans 8:35, 37-39...

LOVES us...

46

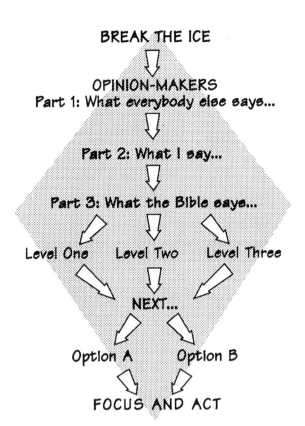

BREAK THE ICE
↓
OPINION-MAKERS
Part 1: What everybody else says...
↓
Part 2: What I say...
↓
Part 3: What the Bible says...
Level One   Level Two   Level Three
NEXT...
Option A   Option B
FOCUS AND ACT

We want our young people to...

■ know that sex is part of God's creation, which He intended for our pleasure

■ be absolutely clear about God's guidelines for sexual behaviour

■ be aware that society, the media and some of their peers will be following a different pattern - and that there will be pressure to do the same!

5. A more Excellent Way

Break the ice

The idea is... to get the young people to begin to think about who influences their opinions about sex - and how.

YOU WILL NEED
To brief 4 or 5 young people
A cassette player

In advance, ask 4 or 5 young people to record onto tape a recent song which contains something about romantic or sexual love. Ask them also to write the lyrics out large on a piece of paper (and not to mention which song they have chosen to other group members before the session!)

1. **EITHER** Karaoke - have extroverts sing to the songs as they are played on the tape,

   OR Guess - have the young person who has chosen the song read out the lyrics, line by line - ask the rest of the group to try to identify the song, and play it (or part of it) once they have guessed correctly.

2. Display all the lyrics.

3. Have a short discussion, asking along the following lines:

   ~ *What do these songs have to say about love/sex?*

Opinion-makers

The idea is... to help the young people reflect on general attitudes to sexual behaviour, identify their own opinions and then become aware of where these might be different from God's 'more excellent way'.

PART 1: What everybody else says

YOU WILL NEED

To prepare the
   statements
Suitable pens

In advance, write the statements from the OPINION-MAKERS sheet (page 52) on a large piece of paper, board or OHP acetate, so that the whole group can see them.

1. Go through the statements one by one, asking the group to decide whether most young people of their age would AGREE, DISAGREE or be UNSURE - take a majority vote and write the verdict by each statement.

2. Talk together as a group about:

   ➤ where young people in general get their ideas about what is right and what is wrong as far as sexual behaviour is concerned,
   ➤ what is 'normal' according to TV programmes, teenage magazines etc. -be specific!

PART 2: What I say

YOU WILL NEED

To make copies
Pens

In advance, make copies of the OPINION-MAKERS sheet on page 52), enough for one per person.

3. Give everyone a copy of the OPINION-MAKERS sheet and a pen.

4. Ask the young people to complete the top half of the sheet with their own opinions - make it clear at the outset that no-one else will see what they have written!

5. Ask the young people to fold down this part of the sheet, so that only the bottom half is visible.

PART 3: What the Bible says

...BE REALLY CAREFUL to be positive and upbeat about this section - we want guidelines to come across as the most excellent way to enjoy one of His great gifts and not as a 'big stick' waved by 'killjoy' Christians!

Level One

YOU WILL NEED

To prepare a
   summary

In advance, work out a very short summary of what the Bible teaches about sex (ie it is intended for a man and a woman in a loving, life-long marriage relationship), using your imagination in its presentation and language your young people will easily understand! Write this out on poster-sized paper, a board or OHP acetate.

➡

6. Simply display the summary and ask your young people what they think about it.

7. In pairs or small groups, ask the young people to use the summary to fill in the bottom half of the OPINION-MAKERS sheet.

8. Bring the whole group together again and go quickly through all the statements, asking what the young people decided about each one.

go to NEXT...

Level Two

YOU WILL NEED

To write out the verses
Blu-tack
Pens
A large piece of paper OR OHP acetate
Suitable pens

In advance, write out the text of some Bible verses which reveal God's guidelines for sexual behaviour, such as:

Exodus 20:14
Proverbs 5:15, 18-19 & 6:32
Song of Songs (selected parts!)
Matthew 19:3-6
John 8:3-11 (selected parts!)

Use separate pieces of card or paper - and colour if possible! You may also wish to add simple explanations of words like 'adultery' and 'Pharisee'. Tack the verses and explanations around the walls of your meeting room before the young people arrive.

6. Ask your young people to walk around the room, reading the verses tacked around the walls and using them to complete the bottom half of the OPINION-MAKERS sheet.

go to Level Three, point 7

Level Three

YOU WILL NEED

To write out the references
Bibles
Pens
A large piece of paper OR OHP acetate
Suitable pens

In advance, write out the references of some Bible verses which reveal God's guidelines for sexual behaviour, such as:

Exodus 20:14
Proverbs 5:15, 18-19 & 6:32
Song of Songs (selected parts!)
Matthew 19:3-6
John 8:3-11 (selected parts!)
1 Corinthians 6:13b & 19-20
Colossians 3:1-5
1 Thessalonians 4:3

Use separate pieces of card or paper - and colour if possible! You may also wish to add clear definitions of words like 'adultery' and 'immorality' - a lot of young people will not be quite sure about what they mean! Tack the verses and definitions around the walls of your meeting room before the young people arrive.

6. Ask your young people to walk around the room, looking up the references tacked around the walls and using them to complete the bottom half of the OPINION-MAKERS sheet.

7. Bring the whole group back together again and go quickly through all the statements, asking what the young people decided about each one.

8. Now ask your group to come up with a short summary statement of exactly what God is saying about sex - clear up any misunderstandings at this stage before you move on!

9. When you have a statement the whole group agrees with, write it on a large piece of paper or OHP acetate - display it for the rest of this session (and the next!)

Next...

Choose the activity which would best suit your group!

Option A: Debate

YOU WILL NEED
To brief leaders/
  young people/
  guests
To familiarise
  yourself with the
  background
  material

In advance, prepare 2 or 3 young people, leaders, or guests to speak positively about God's guidelines for sexuality - BE SURE TO CHOOSE PEOPLE WHO HAVE CREDIBILITY WITH YOUR GROUP!!!

1. Hold a debate around the motion:

   'God's guidelines for sexual behaviour are irrelevant in the 1990's'

   Try to stage it with:

   - speakers 'for' and 'against'
   - contributions from the rest of the group
   - a vote at the end

   As 'chairperson', try to ensure that just one person speaks at a time! Introduce the statistics, quotes and illustration from pages 53 and 54 as appropriate.

2. Briefly sum up what the young people have said.

Option B: Group activity

YOU WILL NEED
To make copies
To familiarise
  yourself with the
  background
  material

In advance, EITHER make copies of the sheet on page 55, enough for one per person, OR make one large copy on a poster-sized piece of paper, board or OHP acetate.

1. EITHER in small groups OR altogether as a whole group, ask the young people to suggest reasons why God's guidelines do actually make sense (- a good way into this might be to ask: *which problems would never happen if people followed these guidelines?*)

2. Pool ideas, introducing the statistics, quotes and illustration from pages 53 and 54 as appropriate - please see the completed sheet on page 56 for guidelines!

3. Briefly sum up what the young people have said.

Focus and act

1. Challenge your young people to think of their own 'action plans' for the coming week - offer suggestions appropriate to your young people, such as:

   Will you go out and become more aware of the effects of people breaking God's guidelines?

   Will you think about where your ideas were different from God's guidelines?

   Will you think through the areas where you might find it difficult to keep to God's guidelines?

   If you are aware that you have already 'overstepped the mark'.... will you say sorry to God, ask for His forgiveness (and believe that you have it!), resolve not to let it happen again and ask God to help you with it?

2. Use these guidelines to PRAY for your young people or have a time of PRAYER in small groups...

   ... thank God that He wants the very best for us
   ... thank God that He gives us very clear guidelines about this area of our lives
   ... express to Him anything which we find difficult to accept about His blueprint for sexual behaviour
   ... ask for His help to stick to His guidelines! (to be dealt with in greater detail next session...!)

FOR THE NEXT SESSION...

You may wish to ask your young people to complete the survey on page 61 before the next session, especially if you have a small group!

Bible Base

Exodus 20:14; Proverbs 5:15, 18-19 & 6:32; Song of Songs; Matthew 19:3-6; John 8:3-11; 1 Corinthians 6:13b, 19-20; Colossians 3:1-5; 1 Thessalonians 4:3

Opinion-Makers

Read these statements and mark whether you AGREE, DISAGREE or are NOT SURE!

	agree	unsure	disagree
It's alright to have sex if you love each other and are committed to each other - you don't have to be married	☐	☐	☐
You can go as far as you like before you get married as long as you don't actually have sex	☐	☐	☐
If you are unhappy with your marriage partner, it's OK to look for someone else who will satisfy you	☐	☐	☐
It's a good idea to live with someone before you get married - it helps you see if you are really suited	☐	☐	☐
Your boyfriend or girlfriend has the right to expect you to have sex with them to show them you love them	☐	☐	☐
You can have sex with whoever you choose, provided they agree and that you are not harming yourself or them in any way	☐	☐	☐
It's OK to have several sexual partners in your life, as long as you're faithful to one at a time	☐	☐	☐
Christians think that sex is a 'dirty word' - that you have sex to have children and not for enjoyment!	☐	☐	☐

- -

Read the statements again and mark those which **seem** to AGREE WITH GOD'S GUIDELINES, those which DON'T FIT GOD'S GUIDELINES and those you are UNSURE about.

	agree	unsure	disagree
It's alright to have sex if you love each other and are committed to each other - you don't have to be married	☐	☐	☐
You can go as far as you like before you get married as long as you don't actually have sex	☐	☐	☐
If you are unhappy with your marriage partner, it's OK to look for someone else who will satisfy you	☐	☐	☐
It's a good idea to live with someone before you get married - it helps you see if you are really suited	☐	☐	☐
Your boyfriend or girlfriend has the right to expect you to have sex with them to show them you love them	☐	☐	☐
You can have sex with whoever you choose, provided they agree and that you are not harming yourself or them in any way	☐	☐	☐
It's OK to have several sexual partners in your life, as long as you're faithful to one at a time	☐	☐	☐
Christians think that sex is a 'dirty word' - that you have sex to have children and not for enjoyment!	☐	☐	☐

Stats 'n Quotes

Britain has 45 unwanted teenage pregnancies per 1000 girls and this figure is rising
(Institute of Sexual Research, 1991)

About 8,400 girls under 16 and 115,000 under 20 get pregnant each year
(The Independent, 1992)

1 in 3 teenagers between 15 and 19 who became pregnant in 1989 had an abortion
(Leeds University, 1992)

Each year over 10,000 teenagers or women just into their 20's will be having their second abortion
(Christian Caring for Life, 1993)

"I saw losing my virginity as a career move"
(Madonna)

"Safe sex is a lie... safe sex isn't safe emotionally"
(D.C. Talk)

Every year over 500,000 new cases of sexually transmitted diseases are treated at clinics in the UK
(19 Magazine, 1992)

At least 30 million people around the world could be infected with the AIDS virus by the year 2000. Other Experts think the number could be 110 million.
(World Health Organisation, 1992)

Girls often agree to intercourse because they feel they must or they think they've got to a certain age when they have to do it. As a result, the majority of girls I have interviewed say they regret how they lost their virginity and would love to turn the clock back.
(Dr. R. Ingham, 1992)

"I indulge in casual sex as an outlet, a rebellion from family problems. It's a temporary recluse from reality. I make believe who I am doing it with cares about me"
(Young woman, quoted by Rob Parsons)

"If you lack love, it is difficult to say 'no' when an attractive boy puts his arm around you. What could be nicer than to be close to another human being, even if it is a momentary fantasy?"
(President of the family Planning Association, 1991)

Couples who live together before getting married are about 40% more likely to have divorced within 15 years of marriage compared with those who have not
(OPCS Household Survey, 1993)

1 child in 4 will, before reaching the age of 16, sees its parents split up
(Observer, 1991)

"If we take our faith seriously, then we must realise that God has good reasons, as a loving creator, for calling us to avoid sexual sin. He warns us that if we sow the wind, we will reap a whirlwind"
(Dave Roberts)

[Data supplied by C.I.T.S.]

An illustration -Two circles

1. In pencil, draw a circle in the centre of a piece of paper

This represents **you**

2. Draw another circle next to the first circle

This represents **two lives touching in a close friendship**

3. Now rub out that second circle, leaving the first one intact

Explain that **if this friendship is broken**, there will be emotional pain, but that you will still be whole

4. Now describe the difference when two people enter into a sexual relationship: the Bible says that the 'two become one flesh' (Genesis 2:24 and quoted in Matthew 19:5 and Ephesians 5:31) - draw a second circle overlapping the first to represent this

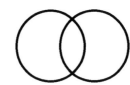

Explain that **the best that God has for us is when the two are completely given to each other**, body and spirit, in marriage (they become one, but still retain their own personalities, like the two sides of a coin) - in sexual relationships outside of marriage we do not achieve God's best!

5. Rub out the second circle, leaving two gaps where it overlapped the first

Explain that **you are damaged when a sexual relationship is broken**, because sexually and emotionally you have become part of someone else

6. Draw 2 or 3 more circles overlapping the first and rub them out

Explain that **if you have 2 or 3 more sexual relationships which subsequently break up, you carry with you a 'broken-ness'**, because you have given something to each partner which cannot be taken back

7. Explain that the **only way to restore 'wholeness' is to come to God in repentance for turning away from His best**, receive His forgiveness and healing, then choose to walk in obedience by keeping the sexual part of relationship within marriage!

Source unknown

54

Why It Makes Sense...

Physical Reasons

Emotional Reasons

Relational Reasons

Spiritual Reasons

To Wait

Why It Makes Sense...

Physical Reasons

- No unwanted pregnancies
- No STD's, AIDS

Emotional Reasons

- No broken relationships
- No risk of feeling guilty
- No confusing love and sexual desire
- No loss of respect for your own body

Spiritual Reasons

- Our bodies are a temple of the Holy Spirit (1 Corinthians 6:19)
- Sex is two people becoming one flesh (Genesis 2:24)
- Because GOD SAYS SO, AND HE IS LORD!

Relational Reasons

- The relationship can grow free from domination by sex
- There will be no comparisons with past partners

To Wait

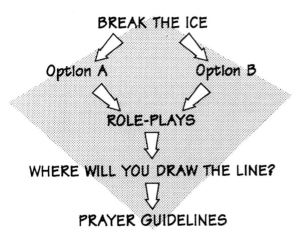

BREAK THE ICE

Option A   Option B

ROLE-PLAYS

WHERE WILL YOU DRAW THE LINE?

PRAYER GUIDELINES

We want our young people to...

■ have some practical help on how to say 'no' to sexual pressure

■ make a firm decision about how they will act in relationships outside of marriage

■ understand that God will forgive us if we have already broken His guidelines, provided that we are honest with Him, are sorry and resolve in His strength not to continue going too far!

6. Where do I Draw the Line?

Break the ice

The idea is... to highlight the many reasons why young people have sex before they get married.

Choose the activity which would best suit your group!

Option A: Active survey

YOU WILL NEED

To make copies
Pens
A large piece of paper OR OHP acetate
Suitable pens

In advance, make copies of the survey sheet on page 61, enough for one per person.

1. Give everyone a copy of the survey sheet and a pen.

2. Have everyone move around the room, asking other peoples' opinions and recording them as explained on the top of the sheet.

3. Bring the whole group back together again and talk about which 5 reasons were mentioned most often - write these up on an OHP acetate or large piece of paper.

Option B: Small group discussion

In advance, make copies of the list of reasons on page 62, enough for one for every 3 to 4 young people.

YOU WILL NEED
To make copies
A large piece of
   paper OR OHP
   acetate
Suitable pens

1. Ask the young people to get into groups of 3 or 4.

2. Give each group a sheet and ask the young people to talk about which would be the 5 most likely reasons why young people have sex outside marriage.

3. Bring the whole group back together again and ask for feedback from each small group - try to come to some agreement and write the most likely reasons up on an OHP acetate or large piece of paper.

if **this would be a little too obvious for your young people...**
Don't give them copies of page 62 - ask them to come up with their own reasons!

Role-plays

The idea is... that the young people think of practical advice to give in some 'real life' situations which link in with the reasons highlighted in BREAK THE ICE.

Introduce this by briefly making the following points, as appropriate to your young people:

➤ God has planned sex for a man and a woman to enjoy within a life-long marriage relationship - anything else is outside of His plan
➤ being in a relationship is OK - but not being in a relationship is OK too! (Quote examples of single people who will present a positive image to this age group - they do not have to be famous!)
➤ when we are in a relationship, it will be physical to some extent - it is our responsibility to work out how physical!

YOU WILL NEED
To make copies

In advance, make copies of the scenarios on page 63, cut them along the dotted lines and select 5 to use with your group.... with Level Two and Level Three groups, we suggest that you use the first scenario (about a young person who has had sex) and then select 4 others.

1. Ask for 5 volunteers.

2. Give each volunteer one of the scenarios and allow 1 or 2 minutes reading and thinking time...

3. ...Meanwhile, ask the rest of the young people to get into 5 groups - station each group at a different point around your meeting room.

4. Now ask one of the volunteers to go to each group and explain his/her situation, acting the part of the character on the slip of paper - the group then has **2 to 3 minutes** in which to give that person practical advice.... with Level Two and Level Three groups, stress that this advice should be in line with God's guidelines!

5. Move the volunteers around after every 2 to 3 minute interval, so that each group discusses each of the scenarios.

6. Bringing the whole group back together again, ask each volunteer in turn to say what advice he/she was given - there may be some humour here, but make sure that there is also some good advice! Open up a discussion about which suggestions were most helpful in each situation, adding comments and ideas of your own as appropriate.

> **LEVEL ONE go to +IF...**

7. End with the first scenario, stressing that God's heart is to forgive, heal and restore, but that in this situation we need to admit where we have gone wrong and to be determined, in His strength, to stick to His guidelines from now on!

8. Ask someone to read **Romans 3:23** and **1 John 1:9**.

 you have a small group or you are not sure whether your young people are mature enough to discuss this without close guidance...
Have each volunteer explain his/her situation from the front, then ask for advice from the rest of the group before moving on to the next.

OR

 there is just a stunned silence...
Have a one minute 'buzz' of ideas in pairs before opening up the discussion - young people are often more confident in making a contribution in front of a group if they have had an opportunity to try it out on 1 or 2 friends first!

Focus and act

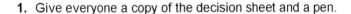

The idea is... that the young people will think through 'how far to go' outside of marriage and, as appropriate, devise practical guidelines to help them stick to God's blueprint.

YOU WILL NEED
To make copies
Pens

In advance, make copies of the decision sheet on page 64, enough for one per person - cut off the 'declaration' section if you feel it would be unsuitable for your young people.

1. Give everyone a copy of the decision sheet and a pen.

2. Firstly, ask the young people to decide how to complete the chart at the top of the decision sheet - **what comes after 'holding hands'? And then...?** How you approach this will of course depend on your young people - one way would be to ask them to talk about it with a partner, then get together with another pair to compare ideas, then ask for feedback to the whole group. (Please see the completed sheet on page 65 for guidelines!)

3. If you possibly can, say how **you** would complete the first and second parts, giving clear reasons for your decisions.... if you would rather not do this, try and find someone who would!

4. Now invite the young people to complete the whole sheet for themselves, **EITHER** on their own **OR** with a friend **OR** in a small group of friends - allow plenty of time for this!

5. Suggest that those who are ready to sign and date the declaration at the bottom do so - others may wish to think further, so do not pressurize anybody at this point!

6. State again that God is always ready to forgive us if we go wrong, but make it clear that this does not mean we should treat His guidelines casually - if we love Him and are serious about following Jesus, we will want to follow His instructions in this important area of our lives!

Prayer guidelines

Use these guidelines to PRAY for your young people or have a time of PRAYER in small groups...

... thank God again that He gives us guidelines because He wants the very best for us
... express to Him (in silence) the decision we have made about this area of our lives or ask for His help to reach a decision
... ask God for His strength to 'stand firm' against all the pressures!
... thank God that He is always willing to forgive, heal and restore - admit where we have gone wrong (if appropriate) and ask for His forgiveness

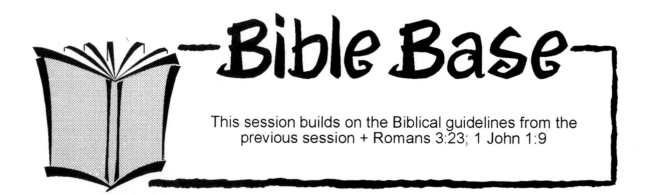

Bible Base

This session builds on the Biblical guidelines from the previous session + Romans 3:23; 1 John 1:9

Why are young people having sex outside marriage?

Survey other young people and ask them to choose the 5 most likely reasons from the list below - shade one box each time one of the reasons is mentioned

I need to be loved

I don't want to miss out on something special

We just got carried away...

There was no one else about - we knew we would not get caught

It's the natural thing to do if you love someone

He/she said "If you really love me, you'll have sex with me"

I want to get some experience before I get married so that I'll know if I'm making the right choice

It's perfectly safe! Nothing will happen to you if you use a condom

Why not? Everybody else is!

My friends said there must be something wrong with me if I didn't

Why?

Decide which of these are the most likely five reasons why young people have sex outside marriage - add others if you think something important has been missed out:

A I need to be loved

B I don't want to miss out on something special

C We just got carried away...

D There was no one else about - we knew we would not get caught

E It's the natural thing to do if you love someone

F He/she said "if you really love me, you'll have sex with me"

G I want to get some experience before I get married so that I'll know if I'm making the right choice

H It's perfectly safe! nothing will happen to you if you use a condom

I Why not? Everybody else is!

J My friends said there must be something wrong with me if I didn't

K ....

....

L ....

....

1. ....

2. ....

3. ....

4. ....

5. ....

You have been going out with your boy/girlfriend for a while now and your relationship has been getting more and more physical. Last night you ended up having sex - you hadn't meant to, things just got a bit out of hand and it seemed impossible to stop...

You have been going out with your boy/girlfriend for over a year now and you're sure you will end up getting married one day! You're beginning to think more and more about having sex together: if you really love each other and are seriously committed to each other, it's natural and right - isn't it?

Your friends seem to talk about nothing but boys/girls! They have started to talk about their experiences too, and, although you try to keep out of it, you're sure they know that you are still a virgin. They have already said that there must be something wrong with anybody who is still a virgin, and you're beginning to think they might be right...

You have been going out with your boy/girlfriend for a while and he/she wants to have sex. He/she has been putting on the pressure, saying things like: "if you love me, you will", "it's only natural - everybody else is doing it", "sex will help our relationship to grow" and "if you won't have sex with me, I'll find someone else who will!"

There's a party tonight and you're invited! The trouble is that, at the last one, there was quite a bit of drink and several couples went off to bedrooms, out to cars and so on... You and your friends were there just for a laugh, but this time you will be going with your new boy/girlfriend...

You've always had the feeling that nobody loves you - your parents have always been too busy having a go at each other to pay you much attention, but it's great now you've found a boy/girlfriend who really does care for you! You're sure that you can show **your** love by having sex with him/her - and that way you might be able to keep him/her too...

It's your decision!

sexual intercourse

First, underline the things you are saving until you are married.

Now, bearing in mind you might have more than one relationship, draw a line downwards to give yourself a guideline of how far you will go:

1. On the first date
2. When you're serious about someone

holding hands

Work out some guidelines which will help you set limits in your relationships - here are some suggestions - use the ones which you find helpful and/or devise your own!

Be upright
Be interruptable
Be accountable

Don't touch the parts you haven't got
Don't lie down
Don't take your clothes off

Be friends with others - don't exclude your friends just because you are going out with someone

Enjoy spending time together with others - don't spend long periods of time alone when physical things can take over

Play it slow - remember that when you've experienced one stage you don't want to go back to the one before

Be balanced in your relationship - don't let the physical side progress faster than other things, like trust, committment and understanding one another

Where will you draw the line in what you watch on TV or in films, or read about in books and magazines?

Where will you draw the line in what you think and daydream?

DECLARATION

I have decided to _____and rely on God's strength to help me stick to this!

Signed: _____   Date:_____

It's your decision!

First, underline the things you are saving until you are married.

Now, bearing in mind you might have more than one relationship, draw a line downwards to give yourself a guideline of how far you will go:

1. On the first date
2. When you're serious about someone

sexual intercourse
taking clothes off
stimulating to point of climax
touching each other UNDER clothes
touching each other OVER clothes
French kissing
kiss on the neck
Long kiss
cuddling
Kiss on the lips
Kiss on the cheek
hugging
one arm around each other
holding hands

①　②

Work out some guidelines which will help you set limits in your relationships - here are some suggestions - use the ones which you find helpful and/or devise your own!

Be upright
Be interruptable
Be accountable

Don't touch the parts you haven't got
Don't lie down
Don't take your clothes off

Be friends with others - don't exclude your friends just because you are going out with someone

Enjoy spending time together with others - don't spend long periods of time alone when physical things can take over

Play it slow - remember that when you've experienced one stage you don't want to go back to the one before

Be balanced in your relationship - don't let the physical side progress faster than other things, like trust, committment and understanding one another

Where will you draw the line in what you watch on TV or in films, or read about in books and magazines?

Where will you draw the line in what you think and daydream?

DECLARATION

I have decided to _____ and rely on God's strength to help me stick to this!

Signed: _____   Date: _____

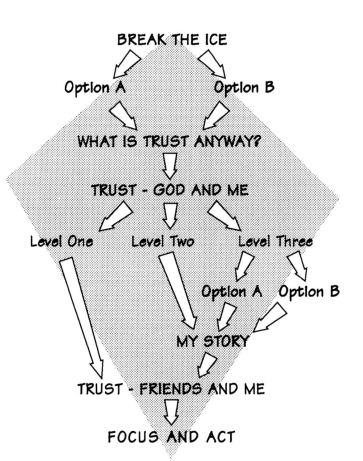

BREAK THE ICE

Option A   Option B

WHAT IS TRUST ANYWAY?

TRUST - GOD AND ME

Level One   Level Two   Level Three

Option A   Option B

MY STORY

TRUST - FRIENDS AND ME

FOCUS AND ACT

We want our young people to...

- ■ know what trust is

- ■ know that God is completely trustworthy

- ■ understand that trusting in Him is an ongoing process and take another step

- ■ consider the importance of trust in friendship

- ■ consider how they might become more trustworthy.

7. Trust

Break the ice

The idea is... that the young people begin to feel what it is like to trust others in a simulation game.

Choose the activity or activities which would best suit your group!

Option A: Spycatcher

YOU WILL NEED
To prepare the slips
   of paper
A container

In advance, <u>cut up</u> <u>some slips of paper</u>, enough for one per person. Write the word TRUST on about 3/4 of them and leave the rest blank. Fold the slips of paper individually and put them in a pot or container.

1. Pass the container round, asking each young person to take a slip of paper, but **not** to tell anyone else what it says!

2. Explain the rules of the game along the following lines:
"Most of you have a word on your slip of paper, which you need to keep to yourselves for the time being - **your** task is to build up the largest possible network of people... if you have a blank piece of paper, you are a SPY - **your** task is to break into these networks!

To start a network, just begin a normal conversation with someone (about what they have been doing this week, for example). When you're ready, include the word on your slip of paper (cleverly!) in a sentence - if the person picks up on the word by saying it back to you in another sentence, you will know that he/she is **not** a SPY and you can make your first link!

Move on to someone else and start another conversation.... whenever you make a successful link, say who is already linked into your network - remember the names the other person tells you and add them to your own list each time (for example, if I have already linked with Jo and now link with Chris, and Chris is already linked with Sarah and Nick, I become part of a network including Jo, Chris, Sarah and Nick!)

If you are a SPY, start conversations like everyone else and try to work out what the key word is - when you have, you will be in a position to break into the networks ...GO!!"

3. Stop the activity after a set amount of time - 8 to 10 minutes would be about right, but be flexible on this!

4. Ask a young person at random to list those he/she is linked with - ask all those named to stand up and then ask any SPY among them to identify him/herself! If the network does include a SPY, it has been infiltrated and broken!

5. Continue until all the networks have been revealed and you can see which is the largest 'unbroken' network - you could add a rule to automatically eliminate anybody who has already been named as part of a 'broken' network....

Option B: Trust activities

There are several well-known activities which involve young people taking a decision to trust, for example:

➤ Have 8 to 10 people form a close circle around one young person, who lets him/herself fall in any direction and is caught and pushed (gently!) around by the others in the circle.

➤ Have one reasonably strong leader and a volunteer! The volunteer stands about 1 metre in front of the leader, puts his/her arms straight out at each side... and falls backwards! The leader is able to catch the volunteer easily by supporting him/her under the arms as he/she falls.

[NB There is a slight risk of injury in these activities, so if you decide to run one (or more) of them, please do take care!]

What is trust anyway?!?

The idea is... to encourage the young people to reflect on their experience of trust and on its importance in relationships.

YOU WILL NEED
To make a large copy

In advance, make a large copy of the discussion guidelines on page 74 on a poster-sized piece of paper, board or OHP acetate.

1. Start by asking for some feedback from BREAK THE ICE:
    [from Option A] *what was it like trying to work out whether you could trust someone or not?*
    [from Option B] *what was it like to have to trust someone else with your own safety?*

2. Now ask the young people to find a partner or form a group of 3.

3. Display the large copy of the guidelines and ask the young people to use them as a starting point for their own 'head to head' discussion about trust - explain that they can choose which questions to talk about and can take them in any order!

4. Bring the whole group back together again and ask for some feedback, perhaps along the following lines:

    ~ *Which of the questions did you choose to answer? Why?*
    ~ *What did you discover about trust?*

5. Draw the threads together, perhaps making the following points:

    ➤ we don't trust everybody!
    ➤ trust often depends on our experience...it's difficult to trust someone if they have let us down in some way in the past!
    ➤ trust is essential in close relationships!

if **you don't like this idea...**
Just use the questions as a framework for a whole group discussion!

6. Explain that you are going on to focus together on trust in two very close relationships - with God and in friendships...

Trust-God and me

The idea is... to enable the young people to focus on God's trustworthiness and on our need to trust in Him and rely on His promises.

Level One

YOU WILL NEED
To invite a guest or guests

In advance, organise an interview with one or two guests who will talk honestly (and in language your young people will easily understand!) about trusting in God - you might choose someone who has a story about how their faith has got them through a really tough time... but stories of trusting God from day to day can also be very powerful! Brief your guest(s) with questions, such as:
    ~ *How can you trust in something you cannot see?*
    ~ *How do you know that you can trust in God?*
    ~ *What difference does trusting God make to your life?*
    ~ *Is it always easy to trust God? ...and so on*

1. Stage the interview(s) in front of the whole group.

2. Open up the discussion by inviting other questions.

3. Begin to turn the discussion round to the young people themselves with questions such as:
    ~ *Could you imagine yourselves being able to trust in God like (guest's name)? Why/why not?*
    ~ *What would it take for you to trust in God?*

If the interviews have sparked off lively discussion, try doing this as a whole group... If not, break into small groups and then ask for feedback.

4. Briefly sum up what the young people have said.

go to **TRUST - FRIENDS AND ME**

Level Two

YOU WILL NEED
To make a large
    copy OR copies
To make a 'promise
    box'
Suitable pens

In advance, EITHER make one large copy of the 'Covenant' on page 75 on a piece of poster-sized paper, board or OHP acetate OR make photocopies, enough for one per person. Also, make a 'promise box' by writing out each of the verses under REFERENCES on page 76 on a separate slip of paper, folding them up and putting them in a container.

1. Introduce this by stating that:

> ➤ you believe in a God who is 100% trustworthy.
> ➤ this isn't just a theory - the experience of many people, today and throughout history, shows it to be true in everyday life!

2. Go on to ask the young people about what makes it difficult to trust God - you may need to begin by being honest yourself!

3. Being careful not to gloss over any of these difficulties, talk confidently about how we **can** rely completely on God and on His promises.

4. Now show the large copy of the COVENANT or give everyone a copy of the COVENANT and a pen.

5. Pass round the 'promise box', asking individuals to take out one slip of paper at a time and then to read out the verse to the rest of the group - decide exactly what God is promising each time and write the reference in the corresponding boxes on the 'form' - please see the completed sheet on page 76 for guidelines!

6. Delete anything which is **not** promised.

7. Ask someone to read out **1 Corinthians 11:25, Numbers 23:19** and **Proverbs 3:5-6** so that you can complete the 'form'.

8. In pairs or small groups, ask the young people to talk about:

> ➤ which promises appeal to them most,
> ➤ which promises they find more difficult to believe,
> ➤ the two promises which had to be deleted, but which some people (some of us?) believe are part of being a Christian.

go to **MY STORY**

Level Three

> **OPTION A: go back to Level Two ...** but make copies of the COVENANT on page 75, enough for one per person, and ask the young people to look up the verses at the bottom in their own Bibles - they can then complete the 'form', either individually or in pairs or in groups.

Option B: People who trusted God

YOU WILL NEED
To prepare a list of people
Bibles

In advance, prepare a list of people in the Bible who trusted God in a particular situation (eg Abraham in Genesis 22:1-19, Mary in Luke 1:26-56 or other characters mentioned in Hebrews 11).

1. Introduce this by reminding the young people that we believe in a God who is 100% trustworthy.

2. Go on to ask the young people about their experiences of trusting God and about how this can sometimes be difficult - you may need to begin by being honest yourself!

3. Being careful not to gloss over any of these difficulties, talk confidently (and very briefly at this stage!) about the importance of trusting in God.

4. Ask the young people to find a partner or get into small groups.

5. Ask each pair or group to choose one of the characters on your list, and check to ensure that not everybody chooses the same one!

6. Now ask each pair or group to read the Bible account and prepare a 2-minute presentation (dramatic, artistic or just spoken!) to show the rest of the group:

   ➤ how the character's trust in God affected his/her actions, attitudes and so on,
   ➤ how difficult it would have been to trust God in that particular situation,
   ➤ how God proved Himself to be 100% trustworthy!

7. See each of the presentations and talk about what we can learn from the character in each case.

My story

YOU WILL NEED
To invite a guest OR be prepared to share something from your own life

In advance, invite a guest to talk honestly and openly about trusting God in their own lives - you might choose someone who has a story about how their faith has got them through a really tough time... but stories of trusting God from day to day can also be very powerful!

1. Stage an interview or just ask your guest to speak.

2. Open up a discussion, encouraging your young people to ask questions of their own!

Trust-friends and me

The idea is... that the young people think about how trustworthy they are in friendships.

YOU WILL NEED
To make copies
Pens

In advance, make copies of the sheet, HOW TRUSTWORTHY ARE YOU???, on page 77, enough for one per person.

1. Introduce this by making the following points, as appropriate to your young people:

   ➤ we believe that God is 100% trustworthy... but we cannot claim to be anywhere near as reliable ourselves!
   ➤ trust is essential in close relationships, perhaps especially in building real friendships,
   ➤ we can work at becoming more trustworthy - our friendships with other people are likely to become stronger as a result.

2. Give everyone a copy of the quiz and a pen.

3. Ask each young person to complete the quiz and then to talk about it afterwards with a friend or friends.

4. Develop this if you can, perhaps choosing from the following alternatives:

   EITHER using the individual quiz statements as a basis, have the young people devise and act out friendship 'dilemmas' which revolve around the issue trust.

   OR Look together at a Biblical friendship (eg David and Jonathan; Ruth and Naomi).

   OR Look together at the very practical advice on friendship contained in **Proverbs 13:20, 17:9 & 17, 18:24, 24:26, 27:6a, 10a & 14(!)**

Focus and act

1. Have a few moments for the young people to reflect on the session... ask them firstly to think about where they are in terms of trusting God:

Level One

Suggest that your young people look out for others who do have a faith and for the difference it makes to their lives.

Levels Two and Three

Ask:

~ *Is there a situation in your life at the moment in which you're finding it difficult to trust God (eg something which looks as if it won't ever change)?*
~ *Is there an area in which you're trusting in yourself or in somebody or something else rather than in God (eg a decision about future career)?*

2. Ask the young people also to recognise how trustworthy they are as a friend and to pin-point where changes need to be made.

3. Use these guidelines to PRAY for your young people or have a short time of PRAYER in small groups...

... thank God that He is 100% trustworthy and that we can completely rely on His promises
... tell Him about a situation in which it's difficult to trust Him...and ask for His help
... admit to Him that in some areas of our lives we trust in ourselves, other people or other things rather than in Him...and ask for His help to change.

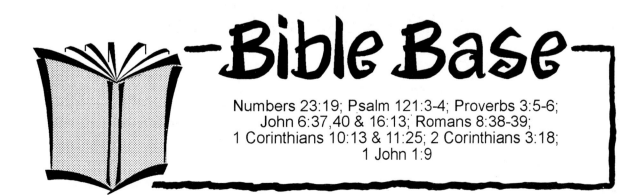

Bible Base

Numbers 23:19; Psalm 121:3-4; Proverbs 3:5-6;
John 6:37,40 & 16:13; Romans 8:38-39;
1 Corinthians 10:13 & 11:25; 2 Corinthians 3:18;
1 John 1:9

What is Trust anyway?

Do you trust... politicians?
police officers?
your GP?
your brother/sister?

Can you say why you do or don't trust these people?

Who would you say you trusted most?
Can you say why?

Can you think of a time someone betrayed your trust in them? You don't have to say what happened if you don't want to, but can you describe how it felt?

Can you think of a time when you let someone down who was trusting you?

In relationships, would you say trust is essential, very important, quite important or not very important? Would your answer be different depending on the relationship?

COVENANT

I, the Lord, on this day, the _____ of the _____ month of 19__, and everyday forthwith, hereby promise you, _____(name) of_____(address) and everyone else who has committed their lives to following me, living or dead, now or in the future:

Reference:

* that I will watch over you and care for you constantly

* that nothing can separate you from my love

* that I will never turn you away

* an easy life, free from all the problems other people have to face

* to transform you into the likeness of Jesus

* to forgive and forget when you own up to me the things you've done wrong

* to provide a way out of situations when you are in danger of breaking my guidelines

* to give you whatever you ask for

* the Holy Spirit to guide you, give you power and reveal the truth about me

* eternal life when you believe in my Son

(*delete as applicable)

SEALED AND DELIVERED_____
_____1 Corinthians 11:25

WITNESSED BY_____
_____
_____Numbers 23:19

ACTION:

Proverbs 3:5-6

REFERENCES

John 6:40   1 John 1:9   Psalm 121:3&4   2 Corinthians 3:18
John 6:37   John 16:13   1 Corinthians 10:13   Romans 8:38&39

COVENANT

I, the Lord, on this day, the _____ **of the** _____ **month of 19__, and everyday forthwith, hereby promise you,** _____(name) of_____(address) **and everyone else who has committed their lives to following me, living or dead, now or in the future:**

* that I will watch over you and care for you constantly

* that nothing can separate you from my love

* that I will never turn you away

* ~~an easy life, free from all the problems other people have to face~~

* to transform you into the likeness of Jesus

* to forgive and forget when you own up to me the things you've done wrong

* to provide a way out of situations when you are in danger of breaking my guidelines

* ~~to give you whatever you ask for~~

* the Holy Spirit to guide you, give you power and reveal the truth about me

* eternal life when you believe in my Son

(*delete as applicable)

Reference:

| P | S | A | L | M | | 1 | 2 | 1 | | 3 | + | 4 | | | | | | | |

| R | O | M | A | N | S | | 8 | | 3 | 8 | + | 3 | 9 | | | | | | |

| J | O | H | N | | 6 | | 3 | 7 | | | | | | | | | | | |

| | | | | | | | | | | | | | | | | | | | |

| 2 | | C | O | R | I | N | T | H | I | A | N | S | | 3 | | 1 | 8 | | |

| 1 | | J | O | H | N | | 1 | | 9 | | | | | | | | | | |

| 1 | | C | O | R | I | N | T | H | I | A | N | S | | 1 | 0 | | 1 | 3 | |

| | | | | | | | | | | | | | | | | | | | |

| J | O | H | N | | 1 | 6 | | 1 | 3 | | | | | | | | | | |

| J | O | H | N | | 6 | | 4 | 0 | | | | | | | | | | | |

SEALED AND DELIVERED _with Jesus' blood_
_____ 1 Corinthians 11:25

WITNESSED BY _'God is not like men, who lie, He is not a human, who changes His mind. Whatever He promises, He does; He speaks, and it is 'done;' -Balaam (+ many others!)_ Numbers 23:19

ACTION: _Trust in the Lord with all your heart. Never rely on what you think you know. Remember the Lord in everything you do and He will show you the right way._

Proverbs 3:5-6

REFERENCES

John 6:40   1 John 1:9   Psalm 121:3&4   2 Corinthians 3:18
John 6:37   John 16:13   1 Corinthians 10:13   Romans 8:38&39

How trustworthy are you???

Can your close friends trust you??? Try this quiz to see how trustworthy you are! For each statement, write ✓ for "YES, THAT'S TRUE OF ME"

O for "MAYBE", "SOMETIMES" or "IT DEPENDS"

X for "NO, THAT'S NOT REALLY ME"

1. If someone tells me something in confidence, I never pass it on   _____

2. I always stick to arrangements I make with friends   _____

3. My friend often turns to me if he/she has a problem   _____

4. I love a bit of gossip!   _____

5. If I'd arranged to go and see a film with a friend, but then been asked to go and see the same film with a boy/girl I really liked.... I would still go with my friend   _____

6. If my friend seems depressed, I find other people to be with until he/she cheers up a bit   _____

7. I'd stick up for my friend if people were rubbishing him/her behind his/her back   _____

8. If my friend was getting him/herself into a difficult situation, with drink or drugs for instance, I'd keep well out of it - it's his/her life after all!   _____

9. If I say I'll do something, I'll do it   _____

10. If my friend asked me to look after something for him/her, I'd be hopeless - I don't want that kind of responsibility   _____

11. If there was something about my friend he/she really needed to know, I would take him/her on one side and gently tell him/her   _____

NOW...turn this sheet round to complete the quiz...

• •

Look back over the statements, and shade in the box which matches your answer...

	1	2	3	4	5	6	7	8	9	10	11
Trustworthy	✓	✓	✓	X	✓	X	✓	X	✓	X	✓
⟨⟨⟨	O	O	O	O	O	O	O	O	O	O	O
Untrustworthy	X	X	X	✓	X	✓	X	✓	X	✓	X

SO... are you basically trustworthy? untrustworthy? neither one or the other??

Look back at the statements for which you shaded a TRUSTWORTHY box... and feel pleased that you would be a trustworthy friend in those situations!

Now look back at the other statements.. can you see how you might be more trustworthy in those situations? Talk this over in a small group.

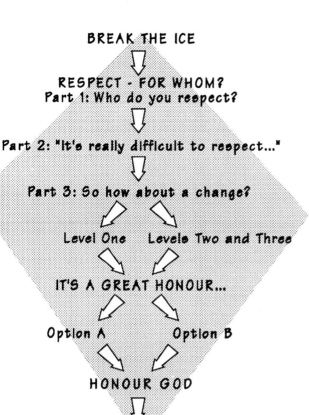

BREAK THE ICE
↓
RESPECT - FOR WHOM?
Part 1: Who do you respect?
↓
Part 2: "It's really difficult to respect..."
↓
Part 3: So how about a change?
↓   ↓
Level One   Levels Two and Three
↓   ↓
IT'S A GREAT HONOUR...
↓   ↓
Option A   Option B
↓   ↓
HONOUR GOD
↓
FOCUS AND ACT

We want our young people to...

- understand what these words mean

- consider who we honour and respect and why

- consider how they might honour a broad range of people

- honour and respect God.

8. Honour and Respect

Break the ice

The idea is... to set the young people thinking about their concept of honour and respect

YOU WILL NEED

To prepare a 'graffiti board'
Blu-tack
Thick, bold pens

In advance, prepare a 'graffiti board' - write the words HONOUR and RESPECT out on a very large sheet of paper (or a strip of wallpaper!)

1. Tack the 'graffiti board' to the wall and, as the young people arrive, invite them to write anything to do with honour or respect on it.

if you think your young people might be a bit reserved about this...
Stand by and encourage the first contributions, offering ideas as appropriate OR perhaps even write a few yourself before the session starts!

⇨

2. Bring the whole group back together again and read out some of the comments on the 'graffiti board': enjoy the witty ones, but try also to make some serious observations about what the **young people** seem to think honour and respect are! Don't say what these words mean to you at this stage!

Respect - for whom??

The idea is... to see who the young people respect and to challenge the widely-accepted notion that respect has to be earned.

PART 1: Who do you respect?

1. Establish one wall of your meeting room as 'DEFINITELY', one as 'SORT OF...' and one as 'NO WAY!'

2. Ask the young people to stand in the middle of the room - read out the following list, one by one:

    ~ *Do you respect the:* **Prime Minister?**
    police officers?
    the Headteacher of your secondary school?
    your tutor at school or college or your boss at work?
    your parents?

(Bear in mind... this needs to be fast-moving!)

After each one, ask the young people to move to the wall which corresponds to their answer and then have some very quick, one-line interviews to find out the reasons for their choice before moving on to the next question. (Some young people may want you to be more specific (eg by stating which parent) - just ask them to react to the first person who comes into their mind!)

(Bear in mind... not everyone will want to talk openly about this!)

3. Now have the whole group go and stand by the 'DEFINITELY' wall - ask the young people to think of someone they really respect and have quick interviews as before, finding out who individuals have chosen and why.

4. Do exactly the same with the 'NO WAY!' wall.

if your meeting room is too small for this OR you would prefer a less active option...
In advance, write the 3 choices ('DEFINITELY!', 'SORT OF...' and 'NO WAY!') out large on a sheet of A4 paper. Photocopy it enough times for everyone to have one each and then cut up the sheet to separate the 3 answers... this will just make the voting process a bit more fun! Give everyone a set of the answers - as you read out the list (see point 2 above), ask the young people to 'vote' by waving the piece of paper which corresponds to their answer. Finish by just discussing the 'DEFINITELY' and 'NO WAY!' categories.

PART 2: "It's really difficult to respect..."

5. Comment that we find it really difficult to respect certain individuals or types of people...

6. In small groups, ask your young people to talk about:

    ➤ what it is about someone (or some groups of people) that makes respect difficult (or impossible!)
    ➤ how a lack of respect affects relationships.

8. Sum up, drawing attention to:

➤ the types of people we find it difficult to respect,
(eg "I don't respect people: in authority
when they fail in some way
who are very different from me
who are less....(intelligent, good-looking, athletic,
outgoing, wealthy, street-wise...) than me
who show **me** no respect!")

➤ the consequences of a lack of respect,
(eg it leads to distance between people and the breakdown of relationships;
it may mean that we don't form relationships with certain 'types' of people in
the first place ...and so on)

PART 3: So how about a change??
Level One

YOU WILL NEED
Note paper
Pens

9. Give everyone a piece of note paper and a pen.

10. Ask everyone to write down the name of somebody they find it difficult to respect.

11. Now ask them to note down:

➤ What good might come out of a change of attitude towards that person?
➤ How they might begin to show that person more respect? (- what might they
stop thinking? saying? doing?)
(You might need to work hard here!! Many young people will feel perfectly justified
in their attitude and will not see any reason to change, especially if the person
concerned genuinely is difficult!)

12. Ask the young people to get into small groups of 3 or 4 and suggest other reasons and
practical steps for change to each other.

13. Bring the whole group back together again and broaden the discussion as appropriate to
your young people: if relationships within the group are characterised by a lack of respct
for one another (perhaps heavily disguised as humour!) bring this fact to everyone's
attention - talk about how your young people feel about this, about what good might
come out of a change in attitude and about how this could happen.

> *go to IT'S A GREAT HONOUR...*

Levels Two and Three

YOU WILL NEED
To make copies

<u>In advance</u>, <u>make copies of each of pages 85 to 88</u>... **read on and guess how many of
each you will need!**

1. Ask the young people to decide which of the following 'types' of people they find it
hardest to respect:

➤ those in authority
➤ those who fail in some way
➤ those who are different from me
➤ those who show me no respect.

2. Group together the young people who find it hard to respect those in authority and give
them page 85, the young people who find it hard to respect those who fail in some way
and give them page 86 ...and so on.

3. Give each group time to work through the sheets **together**:

➤ talking about why particular individuals are difficult to respect (but do make sure that this doesn't develop into one long criticism session!)
➤ looking at the Bible verses and talking about how they might work out here and now
➤ coming up with some practical steps to help each other practise respect.

We suggest that you take a very pro-active role here: it is not easy to pin-point those things which show a lack of honour and respect or to think how to change, especially if the person concerned genuinely is difficult - it's important not to 'gloss over' the problems! A good starting point might be to think about what to **stop** thinking, saying or doing!

It's a great honour...

The idea is... to get the young people to think about the kinds of people we tend to select for special honour and what we do to show this.

(This can be serious or light-hearted... your choice!)

Choose the activity which would work best with your group!

Option A: Altogether...

YOU WILL NEED
To prepare the character profiles

In advance, make one copy of the 'Honours Shortlist' on page 89 and cut out each character profile , or devise your own shortlist by writing the **name** of one well-known person of 4 or 5 of the character types on separate pieces of paper.

1. Ask for 4 or 5 volunteers (but you could manage with 3...)

2. Give each volunteer one of the character profiles.

3. Explain to the rest of the group that they have to decide who is most deserving of a special honour - each volunteer then takes it in turns to say why the candidate he/she has nominated should receive the honour: you may need to introduce a time limit for each 'speech'!

4. At the end, have a vote and then decide on an appropriate 'award' (a medal? a title? something else??)!

Option B: Group discussion

YOU WILL NEED
To prepare the 'shortlists'

In advance, make copies of the honours 'shortlist' on page 89, or devise your own by listing the **names** of one well-known person of most of the character types (adding other 'contenders' if you wish!) and again make copies - you will need enough for one sheet for every 3 to 4 young people.

1. Ask the young people to form a 'committee' of 3 or 4, and then to nominate a 'spokesperson'.

2. Give each 'committee' one of the shortlists.

3. Explain that each 'committee' has to decide who on the list is most deserving of a special honour and what an appropriate 'award' might be.

4. Set a time limit for this - between 5 and 10 minutes would be about right.

5. Ask each 'spokesperson' to report back on the decision reached by his/her 'committee' - allow an opportunity for others to disagree, as appropriate!

Honour God!

The Idea Is... that the young people think about why we honour God, how we honour Him and involve themselves in an act of worship if appropriate.

YOU WILL NEED
To choose
  carefully!
To provide materials,
  equipment, and
  so on

1. Linking back to IT'S A GREAT HONOUR, talk together, as appropriate, about:

   ➤ why we honour certain people... and so why God deserves to be honoured!
     (Exodus 15:11; 1 Chronicles 29:10-13; Revelation 4:11 & 5:13)
   ➤ how we honour people... and how we can honour God **and** how we can dishonour Him!

2. Have an opportunity for your young people to honour God (or to watch other people honouring Him) in a time of worship - you may wish to choose from the following possibilities:

   ➤ visit a church to watch and take part in worship
   ➤ have a walk out into God's creation... the stars late at night can be quite awe-inspiring!!
   ➤ listen to some modern worship songs on tape
   ➤ sing
   ➤ set a Psalm (eg **Psalm 145**) to music
   ➤ re-write a Psalm in your own words or perhaps write a completely original one!
   ➤ dance
   ➤ sketch, paint, model....
   ➤ use material from Taizé or Iona, which may be new to your young people, as the basis for worship.

Focus and act

1. Finish the session with a few moments of quiet...challenge the young people to think about an 'action plan' from this session, offering suggestions such as:

   the focus has been on less-close relationships this time... *will you decide to show respect to someone you find it difficult to honour?*

   Have you become aware that there is little respect in a close relationship you have (for example, with your parents)? If so, what are you going to do about it?

   Are you going to look for more opportunities to honour God in forms of worship - with others or on your own?

Will you turn away, in God's strength, from anything in your life which is dishonouring to Him?

Are you ready to ask God to help you honour Him in everything you do?

2. Use these guidelines to PRAY for your young people or have a time of PRAYER in small groups...

... honour God quietly - remembering that He is worthy of the highest honour!
... admit times when we have not shown honour and respect to Him and to others
... ask to be able to see other people with His eyes
... ask for help to show more respect, even when it's really difficult to do so...

Exodus 15:11; 1 Chronicles 29:10-13;
Matthew 5:38-48 & 7:1-5; Galatians 3:28; Ephesians 6:5-9;
James 2:1-10; Revelation 4:11 & 5:13

It's hard to respect...

People I find it hard to respect are...

Mr. Jones - History Teacher

My lack of respect shows itself when I

say... *what I think about him to anyone who'll listen*

do... *not work in his lesson, talk down to him*

think... *he's a complete waste of space*

say...

do...

think...

say...

do...

think...

Paul wrote this advice to Christians in a society in which slavery was accepted and the occupying Roman army ruled...

*How might his advice apply in **your** situation?*

Slaves, obey your masters here on earth with fear and respect and from a sincere heart, just as you obey Christ. You must do this not only while they are watching you, to please them. With all your heart you must do what God wants as people who are obeying Christ. Do your work with enthusiasm. Work as if you were serving the Lord, not as if you were serving only men and women. Remember that the Lord will give a reward to everyone, slave or free, for doing good.

Masters, in the same way, be good to your slaves. Do not threaten them. Remember that the One who is your Master and their Master is in heaven, and he treats everyone alike.

EPHESIANS 6:5-9

All of you must yield to the government rulers No one rules unless God has given him the power to rule, and no one rules now without that power from God. So those who are against the government are really against what God has commanded. And they will bring punishment on themselves. Those who do right do not have to fear the rulers; only those who do wrong fear them. Do you want to be unafraid of the rulers? Then do what is right, and they will praise you. The ruler is God's servant to help you. But if you do wrong, then be afraid. He has the power to punish; he is God's servant to punish those who do wrong. So you must yield to the government, not only because you might be punished, but because you know it is right.

This is also why you pay taxes. Rulers are working for God and give their time to their work. Pay everyone, then, what you owe. If you owe any kind of tax, pay it. Show respect and honour to them all.

ROMANS 13:1-6

To show honour and respect, I could try...

not to criticise everything he says or does.

getting on with the work,

talking to him more politely.

looking for things which are good about him

It's hard to respect...

People I find it hard to respect are...

My step-brother

My lack of respect shows itself when I

say... nothing - I'm just ignoring him

say...

say...

do... anything to annoy him

do...

do...

think... he's the pits

think...

think...

Jesus taught this to crowds of people on a hillside...

What does it say to **you?**

Don't judge other people, or you will be judged. You will be judged in the same way that you judge others, and the amount you give others will be given to you.

Why do you notice the little piece of dust in your friend's eye, but you don't notice the big peice of wood in your own eye? How can you say to your friend, 'Let me take that little piece of dust out of your eye'? Look at yourself! You still have that big piece of wood in your own eye. You hypocrite! First, take the wood out of your own eye. Then you will see clearly to take the dust out of your friend's eye.

MATTHEW 7:1-5

To show honour and respect, I could try...

talking to him, forgiving him
Looking for things which
are good about him.
Looking for something we
could do together without
getting on each other's nerves.

It's hard to respect...

People I find it hard to respect are...

Jo

My lack of respect shows itself when I

say... *things behind her back.*
hurtful things to her face

do... *get others to dislike her*
as much as I do.

think... *that she's pathetic*

say...

do...

think...

say...

do...

think...

Paul wrote this to Christians in a society divided by race, class, sex, religion...

In Christ, there is no difference between Jew and Greek, slave and free person, male and female. You are all the same in Christ Jesus.

GALATIANS 3:28

*What do they mean in **your** situation?*

...and James wrote these instructions...

My dear brothers and sisters, as believers in our glorious Lord Jesus Christ, never think some people are more important than others. Suppose someone comes into your church meeting wearing nice clothes and a gold ring. At the same time a poor person comes in wearing old, dirty clothes. You show special attention to the one wearing nice clothes and say, "Please, sit here in this good seat." But you say to the poor person, "Stand over there," or, "Sit on the floor by my feet." What are you doing? You are making some people more important than others, and with evil thoughts you are deciding that one person is better.

Listen, my dear brothers and sisters! God chose the poor in the world to be rich with faith and to receive the kingdom God promised to those who love him. But you show no respect to the poor. The rich are always trying to control your lives. They are the ones who take you to court. And they are the ones who speak against Jesus, who owns you.

This royal law is found in the Scriptures: "Love your neighbour as you love yourself." If you obey this law, you are doing right. But if you treat one person as being more important than another, you are sinning. You are guilty of breaking God's law. A person who follows all of God's law but fails to obey even one command is guilty of breaking all the commands in that law.

JAMES 2:1-10

To show honour and respect, I could try...

understanding a bit more
about her.
not saying negative things
about her and to her.

It's hard to respect...

People I find it hard to respect are...
Mrs. Clements.

My lack of respect shows itself when I

say... *ignore her*

do... *ignore her*

think... *she's really spiteful and nasty*

say...

do...

think...

say...

do...

think...

Jesus said this to crowds gathered on a hillside...

*What does it mean in **your** situation?*

"You have heard that it was said, 'An eye for an eye, and a tooth for a tooth.' But I tell you, don't stand up against an evil person. If someone slaps you on the right cheek, turn to him the other cheek as well. If someone wants to sue you in court and take your shirt, let him have your coat as well. If someone forces you to go with him a kilometre, go with him two kilometres. If a person asks you for something, give it to him. Don't refuse to give to someone who wants to borrow from you.

"You have heard that it was said, 'Love your neighbour and hate your enemies.' But I say to you, love your enemies. Pray for those who hurt you. If you do this, you will be true children of your Father in heaven. He causes the sun to rise on good people and on evil people, and he sends rain to those who do right and to those who do wrong. If you love only people who love you, you will get no reward. Even the tax collectors do that. And if you are nice only to your friends, you are no better than other people. Even those who don't know God are nice to their friends. So you must be perfect, just as your Father in heaven is perfect.

MATTHEW 5:38-48

To show honour and respect, I could try...
not let her get to me so much.
smiling at her!
starting little conversations
at first...
concentrating on what's
good about her.

Honours Shortlist

Candidate A

- left school with no qualifications - won the confidence of a local bank manager and secured a small loan - began with a pitch on the local market - a millionaire in 10 years with numerous retail outlets in the region, employing several hundred people in total.

Candidate B

- dived into the sea to rescue a child in difficulty - not a good swimmer and knew the real dangers of being swept out to sea by strong currents in that particular part of the bay - undoubtedly saved the child from drowning.

Candidate C

- many years in medical research - has achieved a notable breakthrough in our understanding of a disease which kills tens of thousands of children every year in the developing world - vaccine against the disease almost ready.

Candidate D

- tireless campaigner for the homeless - gave up a highly paid job in the City to get involved in caring for those living out on the streets - organises and works in soup-kitchens, night-shelters and hostels - responsible for several successful fund-raising initiatives - has brought attention to the plight of the homelss in the local and national press and in government circles.

Candidate E

- very distinguished police career - rose through the ranks to become Chief-Superintendant - several commendations for bravery - service way beyond the call of duty on many occasions.

Candidate F

- well-known singer and record producer - respected internationally for innovative music ideas and high quality concert performances - devotes great deal of time to charity work - gave all profit from a recent record to a famine-relief organisation.

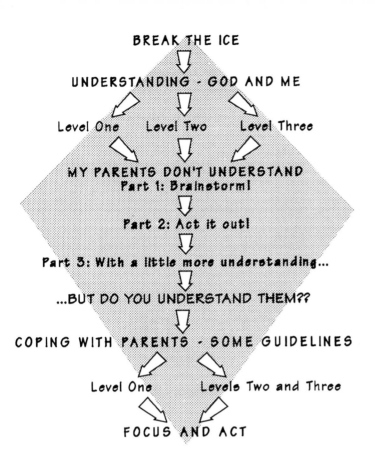

BREAK THE ICE

UNDERSTANDING - GOD AND ME

Level One   Level Two   Level Three

MY PARENTS DON'T UNDERSTAND
Part 1: Brainstorm!

Part 2: Act it out!

Part 3: With a little more understanding...

...BUT DO YOU UNDERSTAND THEM??

COPING WITH PARENTS - SOME GUIDELINES

Level One   Levels Two and Three

FOCUS AND ACT

We want our young people to...

■ consider the implications of being misunderstood

■ know that God's knowledge of them is complete (and deeper than self-knowledge)

■ consider, as appropriate, how to develop understanding in their relationships with God and with others, focusing on their relationship with their parents.

9. Understanding

Break the ice

The idea is... that the young people think about what can happen when there is incomplete understanding in a situation - based on the game 'Consequences'.

YOU WILL NEED
To make copies
Pens

In advance, <u>make copies of pages 97 and 98</u> - guess how many young people will come to this session, divide that number by two and make that many copies of each sheet! Fold <u>all</u> the sheets up to the dotted line so that the section 'WHAT HE/SHE DIDN'T KNOW...' cannot be seen!

1. Ask the young people to get into 2 separate groups.

2. Give the young people in one group a copy each of page 97 and the other group a copy each of page 98 - ASK EVERYONE **NOT** TO OPEN UP THE PART OF THE SHEET WHICH HAS BEEN FOLDED OVER!!

3. Read out the two scenarios and ask everyone to fill in an answer to question 1 on the sheets, then to fold the paper over and pass it on to the person on their right - KEEP THE GROUPS SEPARATE, OF COURSE!

4. Ask the young people to answer question 2 on the sheet they have just been given, fold the paper over again and pass it on...

5. Do exactly the same for questions 3 and 4.

6. Now ask everyone to unfold the bottom part of the sheet, read what it says and answer the last question - they should fold this over again and pass it on for the last time!

7. Each person should end up with a completed sheet, which can now be unfolded and read - have some of them read out to the whole group!

8. Ask for comments from the young people - go on to see if anyone has had a similar experience, which they would be willing to tell the rest of the group about.

9. Conclude that a lack of understanding leads us to make faulty judgements, which can result in wrong opinions or actions and that we need to be aware of this in different relationships and situations!

Understanding-God and me

The idea is... to see how well God knows and understands us, to consider the implications of this and to think about how we can get to know and understand Him better.

Level One

YOU WILL NEED
To prepare the passage
Blu-tack

In advance, prepare Psalm 139:1-16 (or selected bits!):

EITHER write individual verses out large on separate pieces of paper (or wallpaper), using colour if possible - tack the verses in the right order around the walls of your meeting room before your young people arrive,
OR write the passage out on an OHP acetate,
OR ask one or two young people to just read it.

1. Introduce this by asking the young people to think who knows and understands them best...

2. Present the Psalm.

3. Lead into a discussion in small groups - perhaps start by asking: *according to the Psalm, in fact it's God who knows and understands us best... how do you feel about this?*

4. Ask for feedback and briefly sum up what the young people have said.

| go to "MY PARENTS DON'T UNDERSTAND ME...." |

Level Two

YOU WILL NEED
To prepare the passage and the questions

In advance, make copies of Psalm 139:1-16 from page 99, enough for one for every 3 young people you are expecting at your session. Cut each copy along the dotted lines, shuffle the verses and keep each set together in an envelope or with a paper clip. Also, prepare the questions on page 100, writing them out on paper large enough for everyone to see or on an OHP acetate.

1. Ask the young people to get into groups of 3 or 4 and to say who they think knows and understands them best...

2. Give each group the shuffled Psalm and ask the young people to put the verses in the right order (so that they can understand the whole passage!)

> **go to Level Three, point 3**

Level Three

YOU WILL NEED
To prepare the
   questions
Bibles

In advance, prepare the questions on page 100, writing them out on paper large enough for everyone to see or on an OHP acetate.

1. Ask the young people to get into groups of 3 or 4 and to say who they think knows and understands them best...

2. Ask them to find **Psalm 139:1-16** in their Bibles...

3. ...now ask them to answer the questions!

4. Open the discussion to the whole group, focusing particularly on the last two ('to talk over') questions - ask the young people how to go about getting to know and understand God better, adding practical suggestions for prayer, Bible study, learning from others.... as appropriate.

My parents don't understand me

The idea is... that the young people think about the most likely causes of conflict between them and their parents and how greater understanding (on both sides!) might help.

(Be careful not to talk as if everyone lives with both natural parents.)

PART 1: Brainstorm!

YOU WILL NEED
1 or 2 large sheets
   of paper
A thick, bold pen
Blu-tack

1. Begin by pointing out that misunderstanding is very common in relationships between young people and their parents.

2. Go on to make the point that some young people have to live with extremely difficult situations at home - some suffer violence, abuse, bullying and emotional neglect at the hands of a parent, step-parent or guardian.... Explain that you plan to look at more usual, less serious issues and offer help after the session for anybody with a particular problem - DON'T ASSUME THAT THIS WILL NOT APPLY TO YOUR YOUNG PEOPLE!!

3. Ask the young people to shout out as many things which cause conflict between them and their parents as they can think of: as each one is mentioned, note it down on a large sheet of paper - typical issues are tidiness, helping around the house, clothes and hair styles, and arguing with brothers and sisters.

PART 2: Act it out

4. Ask the young people to find a partner (or form a group of 3).

5. Ask each pair (or threesome) to decide which one of them will take the role of a parent and which will play him/herself!

6. Now ask each pair (or threesome) to **EITHER** select one of the issues raised in the 'BRAINSTORM' and act out a typical conversation between a parent and a young person about that issue **OR** to re-enact a real experience.

 you have time...
Have the young people swap over roles, choose another issue and act out a second conversation.

PART 3: With a little more understanding...

7. Ask some of the pairs to 're-play' their conversations in front of the whole group - stop them when the disagreement is in full swing!

8. After each performance, open up a discussion with the whole group, along the following lines:

   ~ *Are there misunderstandings in this situation?*
   ~ *If so, what is the parent not understanding about the young person (about his/her interests, feelings, situation, ambitions...)?*
   ~ *...and what is the young person not understanding about the parent (about his/her interests, feelings, situation, pressures...)?*
   ~ *How could there be more understanding of the other person's point of view? would this help to reduce the conflict?*

(Bear in mind... some young people are coping with huge problems at home...)

9. Briefly sum up what the young people have said, drawing attention to the fact that there is often a lack of understanding **on both sides** of a relationship - acknowledge that parents can be very difficult, but go on to suggest that the young people would gain a great deal from trying to understand more about their parents..!

...But do you understand them?

The Idea is... to encourage the young people to think about how well they understand their parents... and to provide something which might just get some conversation going at home!

YOU WILL NEED
To make copies
Pens

In advance, make copies of the 'SO WHAT DO <u>YOU</u> KNOW?' sheet on page 101, enough for one per person.

1. Give everyone a copy of the sheet and a pen.

2. Ask the young people to fill them in, on their own this time - if they are making a decision about which parent to answer for, suggest that they choose the one with whom they disagree most often!

3. When they have finished, ask the group:
   - ~ *How easy was it to answer the questions?*
   - ~ *Were there things you did not know?*

4. Suggest that the young people take the sheets home with them and try to find out more this week!

Coping with parents...

The idea is... that the young people devise some guidelines for themselves from what the Bible has to say about their relationship with parents.

Level One

YOU WILL NEED
Paper
Pens

1. Ask the young people to get into the small groups again, and ask each group to appoint a spokesperson.

2. Give each group some paper and a pen.

3. Now ask the groups to come up with some guidelines, some 'do's' and 'don'ts', to help young people in their relationship with their parents -allow about 10 minutes for this.

4. Bringing the whole group back together again, ask each spokesperson to read out his/her group's 'guidelines' - have an opportunity for others to react to each set!

5. Open up the discussion, aiming for everyone to reach agreement on a set of guidelines - work on building the third commandment into the discussion (eg *is it important to respect your parents? if so, how can you do this? what would it cost you? what might it mean to your parents? how might it change your relationship?*... and so on.)

> **go to FOCUS AND ACT**

Levels Two and Three

YOU WILL NEED
To prepare the verses
A pot or container

In advance, make a copy of the verses and questions on pages 102 and 103, separate them by cutting along the dotted lines and fold each one - be selective and leave out any which you feel would be too difficult for your young people at this stage. Put the ones you do choose into a container of some kind.

1. Ask the young people to get into small groups again.

2. Pass round the container, asking one person from each group to take out one of the folded slips of paper.

3. Ask the young people look at the verses together and talk about the questions - the questions at the top of each piece of paper are about the verses themselves, and those at the bottom get the young people to think about how they might apply to their situation.

4. After 3 or 4 minutes, ask each group to pass its piece of paper on to the next group - take one or two out and add others each 'round' to provide variety!

5. Move through stages 3 and 4 as many times as you feel appropriate, allowing, of course, groups which get really involved in a particular discussion to continue with it for several 'rounds'!

6. Ask for feedback and open up discussion to the whole group as appropriate.

7. Sum up, acknowledging that there are no easy answers and that, for some young people, this will be an ongoing struggle... you may wish to finish with the following verse:

> *'I will try to walk a blameless path, but how I need your help, especially in my own home, where I long to act as I should.'*

PSALM 101:2 (Living Bible)

Focus and act

1. Have a few moments of quiet to reflect on the session... point out that developing more understanding in our relationships is a process, but that we can take specific steps, as appropriate:

   ➤ encourage the young people to commit themselves to getting to know God better with one (or more) of the practical suggestions about prayer, Bible study and so on from the first section,
   ➤ remind them about the question sheet they have had about their parents -will they use it as a basis to try and build more understanding into this relationship?
   ➤ ask the young people to consider whether understanding is lacking in other close relationships - if so, what can they do about it?

2. Either PRAY for your young people or have them PRAY in small groups or perhaps have a time of personal prayer, based on **Psalm 101:2** or **139:23**.

Bible Base

Psalm 139; Hebrews 4:15

Steve

Steve was meant to be home from the party at midnight. It is now one o'clock. As he opens the front door, his father is waiting for him...

1. What does his father shout?

2. Why is his father angry?

3. What would be a likely punishment for staying out late?

4. What are the consequences of this for Steve's relationship with his parents?

What Steve's father didn't know...

...was that at the party one of Steve's friends had been taken ill and they had called an ambulance to take him to hospital. Steve had gone with him and waited until his parents arrived - they had given Steve the money for a taxi home. Steve's father didn't give him the chance to explain...

If the father had known this, how would it have changed his behaviour towards Steve?

Julie decides to visit her boyfriend at his house as a surprise. As she turns into his street, she sees him coming out of his house with a girl she has never seen before: he has his arm around the girl's shoulder, and they walk quickly away in the opposite direction without seeing Julie...

1. What is Julie feeling?

2. What is Julie thinking?

3. What action does Julie take?

4. What are the consequences for Julie and her relationship with her boyfriend?

What Julie didn't know...

...was that the girl with her boyfriend was his cousin, Sarah, who is several years older than him. She had just received some bad news over the phone and had to go home quickly. As she was crying, Steve put his arm around her shoulder to guide her out of the house and down the road...

If Julie had known this, how would she have behaved differently?

Lord, you have examined me
    and know all about me
You know when I sit down and when I
    get up.
You know my thoughts before I
    think them.
You know where I go and where I lie down.
    You know thoroughly everything I do.
Lord, even before I say a word,
    you already know it.

You are all around me--in front and at the
    back-
    and have put your hand on me.
Your knowledge is amazing to me;
    it is more than I can understand.

Where can I go to get away from your
    Spirit?
    Where can I run from you?
If I go up to the heavens, you are there.
    If I lie down in the grave, you are there.
If I rise with the sun in the east

    and settle in the west beyond the sea,
even there you would guide me.
    With your right hand you would hold me.

I could say, "The darkness will hide me.
    Let the light around me turn into night,"

But even the darkness is not dark to you.
    The night is as light as the day;
    darkness and light are the same to you.

You made my whole being;

    you formed me in my mother's body.
I praise you because you made me in an
    amazing and wonderful way.
    What you have done is wonderful.
    I know this very well.
You saw my bones being formed

    as I took shape in my mother's body.
When I was put together there,
    you saw my body as it was formed.
All the days planned for me
    were written in your book
    before I was one day old

SO...

What does God know about me?
(three things)

Where can I go to be away from Him?

What is God wanting to do for me?
(three things)

How long has God known me?

To talk over...

What difference does it make that God knows me better than anybody else, even better than I know myself?

Is it possible to know God as well as He knows me?

So what do YOU know?

Answer these questions in as much detail as you can about your mum OR dad OR step-mum OR step-dad OR foster-mum OR foster-dad...

How does he/she spend his/her day when you are at school, college or work?

What does he/she like doing best:
- on his/her own

- with friends

- with the family?

What makes him/her angry? Can you say why these things make him/her angry?

If he/she could change one thing about you, what would that be?

Is he/she under pressure at the moment? What from?

Does he/she have fears? What sort of things make him/her fearful? Do you know why that is?

▶ Why should 'children' obey their parents?

Children, obey your parents as the Lord wants, because this is the right thing to do. The command says, "Honour your father and your mother." This is the first command that has a promise with it - "Then everything will be well with you, and you will have a long life on the earth."

EPHESIANS 6:1-4

▶ How easy would this be for you?

▶ What advice is there here for young people?
▶ Does this just apply until they reach adulthood?

My son, keep your father's commands, and do not forget your mother's teaching. Keep their words in mind for ever as though you had them tied around your neck. They will guide you when you walk. They will guard you when you sleep. They will speak to you when you are awake. These commands are like a lamp; this teaching is like a light. And the correction that comes from them will help you have life.

PROVERBS 6:20-23

▶ What do you think about this guidance?

▶ What are young people being asked here to do?

Listen to your father, who gave you life, and do not forget your mother when she is old. (......) Make your father and mother happy; give your mother a reason to be glad.

PROVERBS 23:22,25

▶ How do you feel about doing the last part yourself?
▶ How could you do it if you wanted to?

▶ What does this tell us about Jesus' feelings about His mother?

Standing near his cross were Jesus' mother, his mother's sister, Mary the wife of Clopas, and Mary Magdalene. When Jesus saw his mother and the follower he loved standing nearby, he said to his mother, "Dear woman, here is your son." Then he said to the follower, "Here is your mother." From that time on, the follower took her to live in his home.

JOHN 19: 25-27

▶ When should we stop caring for our parents?

► What responsibilities do fathers (and mothers!) have before God?

Fathers, do not nag your children. If you are too hard to please, they may want to stop trying.

COLOSSIANS 3:21

Fathers, do not make your children angry, but raise them with the training and teaching of the Lord.

EPHESIANS 6:4

► How might this help you?

► How old would you guess the son referred to here is?
► What punishment was there for such behaviour in Old Testament times?!!

If someone has a son who is stubborn, who turns against his father and mother and doesn't obey them or listen when they correct him, his parents must take him to the elders at the city gate. They will say to the leaders, "Our son is stubborn and turns against us. He will not obey us. He eats too much, and he is always drunk." Then all the men in his town must throw stones at him until he dies. Get rid of the evil among you, because then all the people of Israel will hear about this and be afraid.

DEUTERONOMY 21:18-21

► What do you think about this?

► How was Gideon disobedient to his father?

That same night the LORD said to Gideon, "Take that bull that belongs to your father and a second bull seven years old. Pull down your father's altar to Baal, and cut down the Asherah idol beside it. Then build an altar to the LORD your God with its stones in the right order on this high ground. Kill and burn a second bull on this altar, using the wood from the Asherah idol." So Gideon got ten of his servants and did what the LORD had told him to do. But Gideon was afraid that his family and the men of the city might see him, so he did it at night, not in the daytime.

JUDGES 6:25-27

► Given that elsewhere in the Bible we are asked to obey our parents, what do you think of what Gideon did here ?
► Would it ever be right for you to disobey your parents?

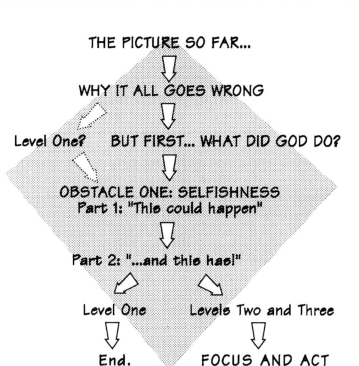

THE PICTURE SO FAR...

⬇

WHY IT ALL GOES WRONG

⬇

Level One?   BUT FIRST... WHAT DID GOD DO?

⬇

OBSTACLE ONE: SELFISHNESS
Part 1: "This could happen"

⬇

Part 2: "...and this has!"

Level One   Levels Two and Three

⬇   ⬇

End.   FOCUS AND ACT

We want our young people to...

■ review the main themes covered so far, assessing where they are in their relationships

■ consider why relationships go wrong

■ appreciate how God mended the relationship <u>we</u> broke with Him

■ draw lessons from this in working out how to mend broken relationships with other people

■ consider how selfishness is a problem in relationships of all kinds.

10. Help! Part 1

The picture so far...

The idea is... that the young people have an opportunity to see how the themes they have been considering fit together and to see where they have got to in their own relationships.

YOU WILL NEED
To make copies

<u>In advance, make copies of the 'warp and weft' sheet on page 111, enough for one per person.</u>

1. Give everyone a copy of the 'warp and weft' sheet and a pen.

2. In each 'thread' down the left hand side, ask the young people to write someone they are in relationship with (eg mum, dad, best friend...and so on) -encourage them to:

   ➤ take a broad view,
   ➤ group people together if appropriate (eg teachers),
   ➤ think where to draw the line (eg by not listing **all** their distant relatives!)

3. Draw attention to the 'warp and weft' as an illustration of how the themes LOVE, TRUST, HONOUR & RESPECT and UNDERSTANDING come into all our relationships - this should, hopefully, already have emerged from previous sessions!

⇨

4. Go on to ask the young people to devise 4 symbols - one for 'really good', one for 'good...', one for 'could be better' and one for 'big problems!' (eg ☆☆ ☆ ✗ ✗✗)

5. Now ask the young people to go through the sheet quite quickly, using these symbols to show how they feel about each aspect of each relationship.... a sample sheet is provided on page 112 for your guidance!

6. **EITHER** in pairs **OR** individually, ask the young people to look at the whole picture and decide:

➤ where it is 'strong', ie things are really good across a relationship or down a theme,
➤ where it is 'torn', ie there are problems across a relationship or down a theme.

7. Ask your young people to keep hold of these sheets for the time being...

Why it all goes wrong...

The idea is... that the young people think about what causes difficulties in relationships.

YOU WILL NEED

4 large sheets of paper
Thick, bold pens (different colours if possible)
Blu-tack

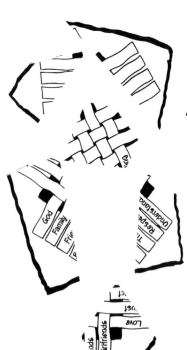

1. Ask the young people to get into 4 groups.

2. Give each group a large sheet of paper and a thick, bold pen.

3. Ask the young people to think, talk and note down ideas as follows:

Group 1 - what makes it difficult to LOVE someone and why LOVE breaks down
Group 2 - what makes it difficult to TRUST someone and why TRUST breaks down
Group 3 - what makes it difficult to HONOUR & RESPECT someone and why HONOUR & RESPECT break down
Group 4 - what makes it difficult to UNDERSTAND someone and why UNDERSTANDING breaks down

Allow between 5 and 10 minutes for this.

4. Have the sheets tacked up side by side on the wall and try to identify things which link with each other (eg groups 2 and 3 might both have highlighted how difficult it is to TRUST **and** RESPECT someone who has let them down in the past) - draw lines to link things together on the separate sheets, using different coloured pens for each link if you have them.

We think that the main links will probably be:

SELFISHNESS:
one person always putting his/her own wants/desires/interests before those of the other

WRONG EXPECTATIONS:
one person expecting too much from another or from the relationship

POOR COMMUNICATION

A LACK OF FORGIVENESS:
mistakes and failings not properly dealt with This material now goes on to consider these four key areas!

LEVEL ONE... It may well be inappropriate to present the gospel message to your young people as suggested below... *if so, go to OBSTACLE ONE - SELFISHNESS*

But first... What did God do?

Levels Two and Three

The idea is... that the young people consider how Jesus mended the relationship between God and humankind and then go on to apply something of this pattern to their own relationships.

YOU WILL NEED

To write out the <u>verse</u>

Blu-tack or an OHP

To prepare the 'presentation' and a suitable opportunity to respond

In advance, write <u>Colossians 1:21-22</u> onto a large sheet of paper or OHP acetate. Also, decide how you are going to present the story of Jesus' arrest, death and resurrection and make the appropriate arrangements:

EITHER show the relevant sections from 'Jesus of Nazareth' or 'Jesus - the Life that changed History'

OR have **Luke 22:47-53 & 63-24:7** read out, asking individual young people to each take a role, if possible. (You might consider using *'The Dramatised Bible'* (Marshall Pickering/ Bible Society) for a change!)

1. Display the verse, without saying anything about it...

2. Making a link with the previous section, begin by reminding your young people how the relationship between God and humankind was broken.

3. Show the video or have the Bible account read out.

PART 1

4. Talk, in simple terms, about what these events mean for us and for our relationship with God.

5. Have an appropriate opportunity to respond, for example:

➤ a booklet (*'Journey into Life'* by N.Warren OR *'Why Jesus'* by N.Gumbel) to take away and read
➤ in song (MP=*Mission Praise*; SF=*Songs of Fellowship*)
  ~ Come and see (MP 85; SF 67)
  ~ From heaven You came (MP 162; SF 120)
  ~ Hallelujah, my Father (MP 206; SF 152)
  ~ Led like a Lamb (MP 402; SF 322)
  ~ Meekness and majesty (MP 465; SF 390)
  ~ You laid aside Your majesty (MP 795; SF 633)
➤ in prayer, perhaps in thankfulness for what it cost Jesus to repair the relationship we broke in the first place...

Wait until you are sure that this has had an impact, then move on.......

PART 2

YOU WILL NEED
A large piece of
    paper OR OHP
    acetate
Suitable pens

(We thought that this part was really important... please don't move on until you are sure that your young people have understood the challenge!)

6. Ask the young people to get into pairs or small groups.

7. Ask: *how did Jesus react to the various people involved in His arrest and crucifixion?*

8. Bring the whole group back together again and have some feedback, noting down the main points on a large piece of paper or OHP acetate.

9. Continue the discussion, drawing out in particular what we can apply to our own lives when relationships go wrong - these guidelines may be helpful:

   ➤ throughout the Bible, God's longing to mend the broken relationship with human beings is very clear.... *but what about us? Are we sometimes happy for a broken relationship to stay broken (because we don't believe things can ever be any different, we think we might 'lose face', or, in a strange way, we quite enjoy the drama...)?*

   ➤ although it was God who was wronged, He was the One who took the initiative in mending the relationship... *should we always take steps to patch up disagreements, rather than expecting the other person to 'make the first move'?*

   ➤ He did this, even though he knew there would be hurt and pain involved... *should we?*

   ➤ He looked at people themselves - not at what they had done wrong... *are we sometimes in danger of letting the problem become more important than the person?*

   ➤ Jesus forgave those who hurt Him... *can we?*

Obstacle One - selfishness

The Idea is... to raise awareness of the consequences of selfishness in relationships of all kinds and of how this might be eliminated from our own relationships.

PART 1: "This could happen..."

1. Ask the young people to get into small groups - anything between 2 and 6 would be fine!

2. Ask each group to act out a situation in which someone is being really selfish. Explain that the groups do not need to think of an ending for their 'sketch' - you will be asking them to 'freeze' the action at a suitably dramatic point!

if **you would like to ensure that a broad range of situations is covered...**
Ask 1/3 of the groups to think on a **world** level, 1/3 on a **community** level and 1/3 on a **personal** level.

3. Have the groups 'perform' their sketches - as the action is 'frozen' each time, open up a discussion among the rest of the young people:

~ *What do you think will happen next?*
~ *What are the consequences of selfishness in this situation?*

Keep this moving quite quickly...

PART 2: "...and this has!"

YOU WILL NEED
Plenty of paper
Pens

1. Give everyone a piece of paper and a pen.

2. Ask the young people firstly to fold the paper to make 3 sections.

3. Now ask them to note down in **each** section ONE time they remember being selfish or experiencing selfishness...

4. ...Then ask them to note down what the consequences of that selfishness were in each case...

5. ...And finally how it could have been different [NB do encourage realism here - it's very easy to think of trite and unrealistic solutions to problems after the event!]

6. In pairs or small groups, encourage the young people to talk about these experiences.

7. Bringing the whole group back together again, briefly sum up what the young people have said, asking in particular for clear ideas on how to squash selfishness in ourselves (eg consider others first; take the initiative; take responsibility... and so on).

> *LEVEL ONE... End.*

Focus and act

Try a short, reflective exercise...

1. Ask the young people to sit straight, close their eyes and take five slow, deep breaths, concentrating just on the air moving in and out of their bodies...

2. Now ask them to think back to the account of Jesus' death and resurrection they saw/ heard earlier in the session - ask them to picture themselves in a garden, at night... what can they hear? Can they see anything in the darkness? Do they feel warm or cool or....?

3. Using your imagination, go on to describe the scene as Jesus and His disciples arrive, in such a way that the young people are encouraged to picture it for themselves.

4. Now ask the young people to run through the events which followed in their imagination - Jesus' arrest... His trial... His crucifixion... His resurrection...

5. Individuals are likely to come to a fresh appreciation of what Jesus went through for us if they are allowed time to do this properly - after a suitable period of time, encourage the young people to move from just watching to saying something in their hearts to God.

NOW...

6. Read **Philippians 1:1-11**.

7. Ask the young people to move on to picture in their minds people they are in relationship with - parents, brothers and sisters, friends... and so on.

8. Encourage them to think about whether they have been selfish in their relationships with any of these people, then to ask for and receive God's forgiveness.

9. Suggest that they now make a firm decision before God to get rid of selfishness and ask for the Holy Spirit's power to do it - do make sure that the young people understand that a firm decision alone will not be enough to bring about change!

if **you have doubts that your young people will be able to take this seriously...**
Try it anyway, but be sensitive enough to move on to the next stage. Having said that, don't panic at the first giggle - it often takes a while to get really involved in this sort of exercise!

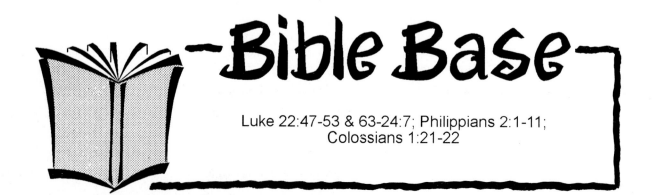

Luke 22:47-53 & 63-24:7; Philippians 2:1-11;
Colossians 1:21-22

	Love	Trust	Honour & Respect	Under-stand-ing
Dad	☆	☆☆	☆	xx
Mum	☆☆	☆☆	☆	☆
Jo (sister)	X	X	X	X
Mark	!	☆☆	☆☆	☆☆
Jon	!	☆	☆	☆☆
Emma	☆☆	☆☆	☆☆	☆
Tutors	X	X	xx	xx
Youth Leaders	☆	☆☆	X	☆
Grand-dad	xx	xx	xx	xx

We want our young people to...

■ consider how wrong expectations, poor communication and a lack of forgiveness are problems in relationships of all kinds

■ receive some training in listening skills

■ take some definite steps in forgiving others and receiving forgiveness themselves.

11. Help! Part 2

Obstacle Two - wrong expectations

PART 1: Break the ice

The idea is... that the young people realise how many assumptions they make about a person based on how he/she looks.

YOU WILL NEED
To select interesting photos

In advance, cut out a selection of <u>photographs</u> of <u>unknown</u> people from newspapers and magazines, making sure you have a good cross-section of ages and 'types' - you will need between 4 and 10, depending on the size of your group. Tack them around the walls of your meeting room before the young people arrive.

1. Ask the young people to just wander around the room on their own or in pairs or in small groups....

2. Encourage them to look at each photo and talk about the person in some detail - *what do you think he/she does as a job? What might he/she do in his/her spare time? What might his/her name be? Where might he/she have gone on holiday this year?* ...and so on - encourage use of the imagination!

3. Bring the whole group back together again and look again at one or two of the photos - pool ideas and impressions about the person, seeing if the young people came to similar conclusions as each other...

4. Ask: *how easy did you find it to form opinions about the people in the photos?* Go on to talk about whether we tend to form opinions about others based on hardly any information at all... *do we automatically assume certain things about anybody who... lives in a particular part of town? Dresses in a particular way? Goes to a particular school?* [use examples relevant to your group!]

5. Briefly sum up the viewsd of your young people.

PART 2: Great expectations

The idea is... that the young people look at the expectations which *might* exist in the relationship between a parent and a young person... and then talk about those which do!

YOU WILL NEED
To make copies
Pens
Paper

In advance, make copies of the sheet on page 119, enough for one per person.

1. Give everyone a copy of the sheet and a pen.

2. Ask the young people to complete the first part of the sheet on their own.

3. Now ask them to find a partner or to form a small group to talk through the questions listed on the sheet.

4. Bring the whole group back together again and have some feedback as appropriate.

5. Draw the threads together, perhaps making the following points:

   ➤ we **all** have expectations of people
   ➤ we often form opinions about people before we even get to know them, based on their skin colour, their sex, their age, where they live, what they wear... these expectations are barriers to good relationship (and are otherwise known as prejudice!)
   ➤ we have expectations of the people with whom we are in relationship ...some of these expectations are fair and reasonable and are linked up with TRUST (eg I would expect a close friend to help me in a crisis) ...but some are unrealistic and lead to tension and unhappiness (eg the young man/woman who expects his/her girl/ boyfriend to abandon all other friendships)
   ~ *Where do we need to make changes?*

LEVEL ONE... Check out the sketch on pages 120 to 122 - if you feel that it is inappropriate for your group... *go to OBSTACLE THREE - POOR COMMUNICATION*

PART 3

The idea is... that the young people reflect on what they expect from their relationship with God - and what *He* expects of them.

YOU WILL NEED
To prepare the sketch

In advance, practise the sketch on pages 120 to 122 - you don't need to learn the lines!

Perform SCENE 1 of the sketch on page 120 - we suggest that you move straight on to the next section afterwards without further comment, but you may wish to have your young people talk about the sketch to reinforce the points made.

Obstacle Three -poor communication
PART 1: What was that you said?

The idea is... to focus attention on how important listening is in good relationships.

YOU WILL NEED
A minute timer
Large sheets of paper OR OHP acetates
Suitable pens

1. Ask the young people to form pairs and decide on one of them to be A ...and the other B.

2. Separate the A's from the B's - explain to the A's that they should choose **any** topic to talk about for one minute... and to the B's that they must not listen whilst their partner is speaking!

3. Ask the young people to find their partners again and invite the A's to begin talking...

4. After one minute, bring the whole group back together again and ask the A's: *what was it like to talk to someone who was not listening?*

5. Open up the discussion by asking: *what sorts of things show that someone is not really listening?* Write suggestions up on paper or on an OHP acetate... your final list might include:

   ➤ looking down, away, anywhere else
   ➤ looking vacant!
   ➤ interrupting
   ➤ adding totally unrelated and irrelevant comments (often about themselves!)
   ➤ reacting wrongly (eg 'glossing over' a problem)

6. Now ask: *what could the B's have done to make it easier to communicate?* Again, list suggestions - you may well need to provide hints here, such as:

   ➤ maintaining eye contact (but **not** staring!)
   ➤ using positive body language (eg leaning forward, nodding the head, making encouraging noises...)
   ➤ asking questions to clarify (eg "do you mean...?")
   ➤ asking open questions (eg "how...?" "where...?" "what...?" "when...?")

7. It's time to put this into practice! Have the young people go back into their original pairs and ask everybody to take it in turns to talk for one minute,

   EITHER about their name (if they like it, why they are called it, whether it has a meaning, whether some people call them by other names(!), what name they would choose for themselves....and so on)

   OR about a person they admire.

8. Still in pairs, ask everybody to sum up what their partner said - this is an 'acid test' to see how well they have really been listening, so don't tell them beforehand that you are going to do this!

9. Sum up, making the following points, as appropriate:

   ➤ better communication can improve a relationship
   ➤ good communication is a two-way process - it depends both on the willingness of someone to share **and of someone to listen effectively!**
   ➤ as we really listen to someone we are showing that we think what he/she has to say is valuable and important - this is key in respecting another person.

   > *LEVEL ONE...* You may wish *to go straight to OBSTACLE FOUR - A LACK OF FORGIVENESS*

PART 2: Listening to God

The Idea is... that the young people consider how essential it is that we make time to listen to God and then are aware of how we can do this.

Perform SCENE 2 of the sketch on page 121 as above...

Obstacle Four - a lack of forgiveness

The Idea is... to finish with a reflective exercise in which the young people think about how vital forgiveness is, who they need to forgive and what they need to be forgiven for.

PART 1: Another true story

YOU WILL NEED
To ask someone to give a short account in advance

1. If at all possible, begin with a short account from someone who can talk first-hand about a situation in which he/she has struggled to forgive someone else...and then about the difference forgiveness actually made - you may wish to record this onto an audio cassette and play it at your session, as a visitor will change the group dynamics!

PART 2: If you can't forgive, you can't forget...

YOU WILL NEED
To make a large copy

(Do be sensitive here... people who have been hurt often feel that they are themselves to blame - we need to offer hope that things will change when they forgive, rather than sounding as if we are criticising them for finding forgiveness difficult...)

In advance, make a copy of the question sheet on page 123 - it needs to be big enough for everyone to see, so use a large sheet of paper or OHP acetate. You may wish to miss out the last question.

2. Ask the young people to look through the questions on their own.

3. Now invite them to find a partner and talk about the questions OR to continue to work through them on their own - it's important that the young people **really think** about these questions and don't just rush through them, so make this clear at the outset!

4. Go on to make one or two points about forgiveness as appropriate to your group, inviting contributions from your young people as you do so:

   ➤ when someone wrongs us in some way, we have a choice about how to react to them - it's OK to feel hurt and angry, but Jesus makes it clear that if we let that go on (by refusing to forgive, bearing a grudge or wanting revenge), we are ourselves in the wrong [see **Matthew 6:14-15 & 18:21-35**]

   ➤ if we have been really hurt by someone, we may feel that....

   ....we **cannot** forgive them - but we can with the Holy Spirit's help
   ....we **don't want** to forgive them - forgiving someone can be a process and **wanting to obey** God in this, **wanting to want** to forgive, may be the first step

   ➤ just as a lack of forgiveness poisons our relationships with other people, so not asking for and receiving God's forgiveness for the things we do which hurt and offend Him spoil our relationship with Him

   ➤ if we admit to God those things which we have done wrong, **He will forgive us** - this is a **promise** - we might not feel any different, but the facts are that things most definitely are different! [see **1 John 1:8-10**]

PART 3: Reflective exercise

YOU WILL NEED
Numerous small slips of paper
Pens
A candle in a large fire-proof container
Matches!

5. If appropriate to your group, pray together, asking the Holy Spirit to show each young person the things which He would like to be put right with God and with other people...

6. Give each young person a pen and several slips of paper - put the remaining slips where everybody can easily get at them.

7. In an atmosphere of as much quiet and thoughtfulness as is possible in your group(!), ask the young people to write down on separate slips of paper:

   ➤ the names of anybody they need to forgive
   ➤ (if appropriate) anything they need to ask God's forgiveness for.

   Allow plenty of time for this and make it clear at the outset that **nobody will be reading what anybody else has written!**

8. Ask the young people to fold up their slips of paper and hold on to them....

LEVEL ONE... you may wish to go straight to point 10

9. Perform the final part of the sketch on page 122 as above...

10. Light the candle in the container and put it in a prominent place.

11. Have an opportunity for the young people to add to their collection of slips of paper anything which might have occurred to them whilst they were watching the sketch.

12. PRAY for your young people or have them PRAY quietly on their own.

13. Invite everybody to come and burn their slips of paper in the candle -this is a symbol of those things being forgiven, so encourage the young people to do this only when they are ready (which may not be before the end of **this** session....)

And to conclude...

1. Finish this whole course with PRAYER - PRAY a blessing on your young people and on their relationships, and encourage them to PRAY in small groups individually if you can.

2. Make sure everyone has a 'warp and weft' sheet (see HELP!! - PART ONE) to take away... about three weeks from now, make a point of talking about it with your young people - how have they been getting on??

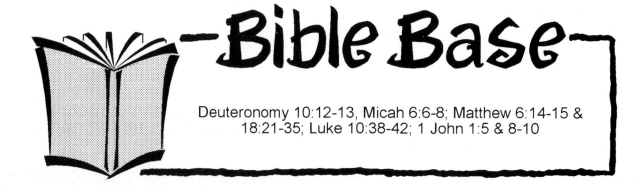

Bible Base

Deuteronomy 10:12-13; Micah 6:6-8; Matthew 6:14-15 & 18:21-35; Luke 10:38-42; 1 John 1:5 & 8-10

Great Expectations

What some parents expect of young people... and what young people expect in return! Have a look through and decide which are fair and reasonable and which are not!!

not to always want your own way

to take my advice - I'm older and wiser than you!

to dress and act in a way which won't embarrass me

not to ask me where I've been, who with, how, when, why...

to approve of all my friends, all my decisions, all I do!

to give me money when I need it

to be like I used to be when I was your age

to care for me

I expect you...

to pull your weight around the house

to be there whenever I need you

to be everything I never had the opportunity to be

to listen to me, but not to tell me what to do!!

to tell me what's going on in your life

to still want to be part of the family

to tidy up for me, do my cooking, wash my clothes...

to let me do what everybody else is allowed to do...

NOW

Find a partner or get into a small group:

► begin by comparing ideas of which expectations are unfair and unreasonable
► then talk about:

- Which expectations your parent, parents or guardian have of you - how do you feel about them?
- What you excpect of them - are you sure you're being reasonable?
- What can you do about the unfair and unreasonable expectations on either side?

LASTLY...

think of another relationship (boy/girlfriend, friend... and so on) - on a sheet of paper, brainstorm the kinds of expectations people have of each other in this relationship... then talk about how fair or unfair each are.

"It's good to pray"

- By Ian M Butterfield

[Based on a series of adverts. in which people are encouraged to use the 'phone with the phrase: "it's good to talk"]

CHARACTERS	**Roger:**	a person praying
	Bob:	an observer

PERFORMANCE NOTES   Bob is an 'invisible' observer in all three scenes - the audience can see him, but Bob can neither see him nor hear him. A cockney accent would make Bob more like the character in the advert....but it's not essential!

COSTUME   Roger needs a shirt which can be buttoned

PROPS

a chair	a pen
2 tables	a candle
a Bible	paper
a bowl	a box of matches
a packet of cereal	a flame-proof container
a small plate with two slices of toast on it	

Scene 1

A chair is placed centre stage - beside it is a small table with a Bible on it

[*Enter* Roger, *he sits down and picks up the Bible and starts to read it.* Bob *enters and examines* Roger, *eventually peering over his shoulder at the passage he is reading*]

Bob: Romans chapter 8 - good choice. [*realising*] Oh, it's alright, he can't see me

Roger: [*reading*] 'We know that in everything God works for the good of those who love Him'

Bob: Have you ever wondered what it would be like to listen in to someone's prayers?

Roger: Dear Lord Jesus...

Bob: ...or have someone listen in to yours?

Roger: ...thank you for what I've just read, for what I've just learned.... and thank you for letting me fail my exam - I know it must be for the best anyhow

Bob: Not very believable, is it? What he really wants to say is this:

Roger: [*angry*] Why, Lord? Why? Why did you let me fail? It isn't fair! When I said I'd follow you, you said you'd look after me - but now you've let me down!

Bob: God did say He'd look after him, but He didn't say He'd be an insurance policy - at least, not the kind he's after.

Roger: Look, it says here: '...in everything God works for the good of those who love Him'

Bob: Actually, that doesn't mean that Christians won't have problems, but that God will help them through them.

Roger: Lord, what good can come from this?
    [*pause*]

Bob: [*realising the audience is expecting him to know the answer*] Well don't look at me. I don't know, do I? Maybe his life would take a different path if he had passed. Maybe God doesn't want him to know just yet. Maybe God just wants him to trust Him.

Roger: [*thinking aloud*] Maybe God just wants me to trust Him.

Bob: The boy's learning!

Roger: I'm sorry I got angry, Lord, it's just that it isn't easy being a Christian these days...

Bob: He's got a point there

Roger: ...so please help me to trust you more.

Bob: It's good to pray.

Scene 2

A chair is placed centre stage - beside it is a small table with a Bible on it and a pair of shoes underneath

[*Enter* Bob. *He looks at the Bible and then at the breakfast items.*]

Bob: Someone told him that it's good to start the day with God. Of course, they didn't know he had a back problem - he can't get off it!

[*Enter* Roger, *wearing no shoes. He is fastening his shirt, but hasn't got the buttons aligned with the correct button holes*]

See what I mean?

Roger: [*without feeling*] Lord Jesus, thank you for this [*yawn*] bright and beautiful morning... [*realising he's doing the buttons up wrongly*] Oh blast! [*he corrects the button fastening*]

Bob: Charming, I must say! It's not very respectful, is it? Not very honouring to God?

Roger: [*goes over to the Bible, opens it, holds it up to read it - it is upside down. He puts it down and then rubs his eyes in an attempt to focus them.*] Lord, please help me to understand what I read...

[Bob *turns the Bible the right way up whilst* Roger *is rubbing his eyes*]

[Roger *picks up the Bible again and realises it is now readable*] Oh, thank you Lord!

Bob: And that's another thing - why are we always surprised when God answers our prayers? We spend a lot of time asking Him for things, but never really expect Him to answer.

Roger: [*reading*] Ephesians 5 verse 14: 'Wake up, sleeper, rise from death and Christ will shine on you'

Bob: Y'know, I think God might be trying to tell him something!

[Roger *yawns and starts to fall asleep*]

Trouble is, he's too dozy to notice. How can he ever expect to get to know God better, when in this state it would take a major earthquake to get through to him?

[*the Bible falls off* Roger's *knee and he wakes up. He looks at his watch and dashes over to the cereal and toast*]

This could be interesting - Snap, Crackle and Prayer!

Roger: [*praying and eating*] Lord Jesus, this'll have to be a quick prayer as I've got to go. You know all the people I'm supposed to be praying for and all their needs...

Bob: Which is just as well 'cos he can't remember any of them

Roger: ...so please bless and help them all. And please help me, Lord, with everything I've got to do today. And please make mum better. And, Lord, please stop it raining on Saturday, because our youth group is going out for the day. And also...

[*by this stage*, Roger *has finished/given up on his cereals. He picks up the toast and takes it to the other table in order to put on his shoes. He puts one piece of toast in his mouth, which temporarily shuts him up*]

Bob: That's not a prayer - it's a shopping list, and not a very good one at that. What about saying "thank you"? Or "sorry"? Don't just give a list - give something of yourself.

Roger: [*finishing the slice of toast*] I ask all these things in Jesus' name. Amen.

Bob: [*picks up the second slice of toast*] First thing in the morning is a good time to be with God, but it's not the only time - for some people, evenings are better. [*takes a small bite of the toast*] It's good to pray.

[Roger *is left looking for his missing slice of toast*]

...continued

Scene 3

A chair is placed centre stage - beside it is a small table with a Bible on it. Also on the table is a candle in a container, some paper and a pen

[*Enter* Roger. *He sits down, picks up the Bible and begins to read it.* Bob *enters and watches. After a pause,* Roger *puts the Bible down, but leaves it open and adopts an attitude of prayer*]

Bob: Sometimes we don't need to say anything. Sometimes it's just enough to be in God's presence. [*pointing at* Roger] He's got a lot on his mind, needs to put a lot right with God. Now that might take some time and it's a personal thing - it isn't right that you and I should overhear the details of what he is saying to God. He's saying sorry to God for all the times he's thought, done and said things which are wrong, for all the times he's let God down. He's asking for forgiveness. And you know what? God doesn't just add these things to a long list of other items to forgive sometime in the future...He forgives them here and now. It's like this: imagine he wasn't just telling God about those things, but he was writing them down too.

[Roger *starts to write on the paper*]

It's a long list of things he's now ashamed of - but it's a list Jesus died to forgive.

[Bob *takes out the matches and lights the candle*]

Jesus said: " I am the light of the world"

[Roger *takes the paper he has been writing on, folds it up and burns it in the flame of the candle.* Bob *watches in silence until the paper burns away*]

Gone. In God's eyes, when He forgives something, it's gone - gone forever.

[Roger *continues in an attitude of prayer*]

Want to know what he was reading? Kind of interesting this - [*picks up the Bible and begins to read*] 1 John 1 verse 5: 'God is light and in Him there is no darkness at all...if we say we have no sin, we are fooling ourselves...But if we confess our sins, He will forgive us... He will cleanse us from all the wrongs we have done.'

[*closes and replaces the Bible*]

Roger: Thank you, Lord Jesus, for dying so that I can be forgiven!

Bob: Well, that's got him sorted. [*blows out the candle*] It's good to pray. It's good to be forgiven too!

When you can't forgive you can't forget!

In your experience, do you find people say "sorry" to you, or do you have to say "sorry" to them?

Think of someone who has hurt you in some way... what difference would it make if this person said "sorry"?

How do you feel when someone says "sorry" to you?

How can you forgive someone who does not say "sorry" to you?

Do people have to deserve forgiveness before you can forgive them?

What are the results of unforgiveness in a relationship? Who would get hurt?

What can we learn from God about forgiveness?

[Please note that the resources below have, with just one or two exceptions, been taken from the extensive listings provided by CITS (Christian Initiative on Teenage Sexuality) - we are grateful to be able to use them here!]

FOR YOUTH LEADERS

...IF you have time, a brilliant, Biblical overview of the whole area of relationships is:

Right Relationships
Tom Marshall, (Sovereign Word, 1992) £4.95

...IF you are looking for teaching resources to build on some of the themes in 'With or Without You?' or to cover some of the themes we have not tackled:

Getting along with Parents
Is Marriage in your Future?
Sex: a Christian Perspective
(Scripture Press, 1990) £6.75 each
Material for 4 more sessions in each booklet.

Pressure Points
Phil Moon & Alan Hewerdine, (CPAS/Covenanters, 1992) £4.50
Of the 10 sessions, one is on homosexuality and one is on sexuality and AIDS.

Teaching the Truth about Sex
David Lynn & Mike Yaconelli, (Zondervan, 1990) £7.99
12 sessions, including some material on the possible consequences of sexual activity outside marriage, ie unwanted pregnancy, AIDS, and STD's.

YOYO 2
Peter Graystone, Paul Sharpe & Pippa Turner, (Scripture Union, 1992) £3.95
5 of the 8 sessions are on relationships (Friendships; Parents; Girlfriends and Boyfriends; Sex; Being Alone.)

YOYO 3
Peter Graystone, Paul Sharpe & Pippa Turner, (Scripture Union, 1992) £3.95
One session on self-worth (8 sessions in all).

Youthwork magazine
bi-monthly, £1.75 per issue
'Ready-to-use' meeting plans have sometimes been on relationships... back copies include sessions on self-esteem, sex and marriage.

...videos:

How to handle the Pressure Lines
Josh McDowell, (Word UK, 1989) £14.99
Why and how to say 'NO' to sexual pressure, with Biblical examples.

Lessons in Love
Steve Chalke (Care, 1990) £11.95
7 x 15 minute talks, addressing some of the key issues from a clearly Biblical perspective, including dating, 'how far to go', masturbation, guilt and forgiveness.

Make Love Last
(Christians in Education, 1994) £39.95
30 minute programme, presenting the case for waiting for sex, without beating around the bush! Originally intended for schools, the pack comes with material for 10 PSHE lessons, but 'Christian' and 'Youth Worker' supplements are also available on request.

Who do you listen to? Sex in the age of AIDS
Josh McDowell et al, (International Films) £14.99
Dramatic presentation of the dangers of pre-marital sex, AIDS, STD's and why to wait. American bias, but works well in the UK.

...these organisations will be able to help with advice and specialist resources:

ACET   - AIDS care, education and training
PO Box 3693
LONDON SW15 2BQ.

CARE for the Family   - Advice & resources on many issues!
53 Romney Street
LONDON SW1P 3RF.

CITS   - Christian Initiative on Teenage Sexuality
(as above)

Courage   - Help with overcoming homosexuality
PO Box 338
WATFORD
Herts WD1 4BQ.

CWR   - Counselling, training and resources
Waverley Abbey House
Waverley Lane
FARNHAM
Surrey GU9 8EP.

LIFE   - Campaign to save the unborn
Life House
1a Newbold Terrace
LEAMINGTON SPA
Warks CV23 4EA.

...continued

FOR YOUNG PEOPLE

How about buying some of these and lending them out to your young people during (and after!) the course?

All Change
Roger Day, (Harvestime Publishing, 1991) £2.50

Emotions, can you trust them?
Dr James Dobson, (Hodder & Stoughton, 1980) £2.50

Families: don't you just love them?
Colin Piper, (CWR, 1994) £4.95

Going Out
Veronica Zundel, (Hodder & Stoughton, 1990) £2.99

HIV - Facts for Life, (booklet)
Available from ACET (see page 125 for details)

Just good Friends?
Joyce Huggett, (IVP, 1985) £3.95

Life in a Sex-mad Society
Joyce Huggett, (Frameworks, 1988) £3.50

Life in the Balance
Sue Williams, (Harvestime Publishing, 1992) £3.50

Lonely Love - Masturbation, (leaflet)
Paul Francis, (Going Public, 1991) £0.50

Love and Sex
Josh McDowell, (Scripture Press, 1988) £1.95

Old Enough to Know
Michael W Smith, (Word UK, 1987) £2.50

Secret of Loving, The, (cassette)
Josh McDowell, (Word UK, 1983) £2.99

Too Hot to Handle
Various, (Baptist Youth, 1990) £0.50